A life
by design

From Brent
15/02/05

To my flamboyant red-headed mother—
the original style queen.

A life by design

the art and lives of
FLORENCE BROADHURST

Siobhan O'Brien

ALLEN&UNWIN

First published in 2004

Allen & Unwin
83 Alexander Street
Crows Nest NSW 2065
Australia
Phone: (61 2) 8425 0100
Fax: (61 2) 9906 2218
Email: info@allenandunwin.com
Web: www.allenandunwin.com

National Library of Australia
Cataloguing-in-Publication entry:

O'Brien, Siobhan, 1971- .
    A life by design: the art and lives of Florence Broadhurst.

    Bibliography.
    Includes index.
    ISBN 1 74114 398 5.

    1. Broadhurst, Florence. 1899-1977 - Bibliography. 2. Artists,
    Australian - Biography. I. Title.

700.920994

Set in 10.5/17.2 pt Palatino Light by Bookhouse, Sydney
Printed by Griffin Press, Netley, SA

10 9 8 7 6 5 4 3 2

Foreword

A life by design is the first publication to visit and document in detail the fascinating and enigmatic life of Florence Broadhurst—singer, banjolele player, painter, business woman, mother and dress and wallpaper designer. I have been asked to comment on Florence's significance as an Australian designer in the context of this biography. This provides a welcome opportunity to place Australian life and design in an international context.

In 1959, when she turned 60, Florence decided to buck the trend and established Australian (Hand Printed) Wallpapers (renamed Florence Broadhurst Wallpapers Ltd in 1969). From the mid 19th century, wallpaper had predominantly been imported to Australia from Britain, as well as from France, Canada and America. Although some effort was made at the beginning of the 20th century to manufacture papers in Australia (Morrison's and Gilkes & Co.), few were produced and few survive today. It is Broadhurst's successful wallpaper design and production venture, as well her reputation as a colourful Sydney personality with an A-list of prestigious clients, and her tragic death in 1977, for which Florence is best remembered today.

Since the late nineties, awareness of Florence Broadhurst's significance has grown exponentially in Australia and overseas. Siobhan O'Brien's article, 'Mistress of the Rolls', which appeared in the *Sydney Morning Herald*'s 'Good Weekend' magazine in 1999, did much to revive curiosity and interest in Florence's legacy, as has the development of the Broadhurst collection at the Powerhouse Museum, and the re-interpretation of Florence's designs as fashion prints by cutting-edge Australian and New Zealand fashion designers. Feature articles on Broadhurst in *Casa Vogue* (Italy) and the *International Herald Tribune* (Paris) have also sparked international interest and appreciation in this Australian artist's life and legacy.

Florence Broadhurst went from humble beginnings to lead a celebrity life, and through her extraordinary determination and charm won entree into 'high society'. Although she was a Sydney personality, Florence Broadhurst was a private person shielding the details of her personal life as this biography and previous articles have revealed. Today, there are almost as many accounts and memories of Florence Broadhurst as there are wallpaper designs and, to some extent, specific details of Florence's life remain unknown and continue to intrigue researchers and biographers, as well as family, friends and colleagues.

What is known, however, is that Florence had drive, vision and marketing acumen. Her tireless charity work, through which she established a loyal and influential clientele, her technology-driven approach to production, the deliberate pricing of her papers to compete with machine-made imports, her highly personalised service and her avoidance of wholesaling, provide keys to her business success. So do the merging of her life's experiences, flamboyant personality and public confidence into a dynamic array of bold, colourful designs.

Sample books in the Powerhouse Museum's collection contain an amazing range of colour combinations from Broadhurst's favourite fuscia pinks through to classic seventies lime greens and vivid oranges to turquoise. Patterns with exotic titles proliferate: Oriental filigree, Japanese fans, Japanese floral, Japanese bamboo, Kabuki, Spanish scroll, Mexican daisy, Persian birds, Birds of Paradise, Large paisley, Florentine and Tudor tapestries. Her hallmark Peacocks design on silver foil is perceived as one of her best mature works—Florence had no hesitation in posing with it in one of her stylish advertisements.

Florence, one of Australia's most prolific designers of wallpapers, which were in their day described as 'Vigorous designs for modern living', became part of a wave of post-World War II retailers, artists, designers and architects, including retailer Marion Hall Best, architect Harry Seidler, industrial designer Gordon Andrews and graphic designer Martin Sharp, who also printed on silver foil in the sixties. This group radically changed Australian attitudes toward design. In keeping with Florence's own personality, her legacy doesn't look like running out of steam soon—rather it appears to be rolling along, full steam ahead with her patterns and designs appearing in fashion, interior decorating and even advertising!

Anne-Marie Van de Ven
Curator, Decorative Arts and Design
Powerhouse Museum, Sydney

Contents

Preface

My interest in Florence Broadhurst began in 1999 when I walked into Chee Soon & Fitzgerald, a diminutive but intriguing interior design shop on Crown Street in Sydney. At the time, I was cutting my teeth as a freelance journalist and just the day before a friend had mentioned in passing that the owners—Casey Khik and Brian Fitzgerald—were redistributing the wallpaper designs of an old woman who had been murdered in the seventies. He thought it might make a good story.

Usually one to be sceptical, I followed a hunch that this was a good lead. I can still remember walking into the shop for the first time: it was a veritable kaleidoscope of colour, filled with Marimekko prints, vintage glass-ware, shag pile rugs and bolts of vibrant fabric. I barely had time to introduce myself before I was perched on a stool out the back of the shop—a cup of tea in one hand

and a Florence Broadhurst sample book in the other. It took a few minutes but I had fallen hopelessly in love.

It was this chance meeting with her wallpaper that led to a full-blown obsession with making sense of Florence Broadhurst's life. I also hoped to reinvigorate interest in her designs and help—at least in some small way—to solve her murder.

I remember feeling (and still feel) driven by a strong sense of injustice for a number of reasons. Firstly, Florence had played a major part in the history of Australian interior design and her contribution had never been fully and formally recognised until recently. And secondly, Florence had died in such a senseless, horrific way. The day that Florence Broadhurst was murdered in her Paddington studio-factory in 1977, the memory of her flamboyant life and her contribution to society had simply been discarded. But to me, Florence Broadhurst was not dead—she was just waiting to be rediscovered.

Armed with the information that Casey and Brian could offer me, I set out on a quest to track down family members, talk to the police from the homicide squad who had worked on her case in the seventies, and interview ex-employees, friends, lovers, acquaintances, business associates and neighbours. It did not take long for the jigsaw pieces of her life to come together. I would talk to someone who knew Florence; they'd pass on a telephone number or an address of someone else who knew her and before long I had a telephone book full of Broadhurst enthusiasts. It was the unlikeliest list: a junky that lived in a decrepit rented flat in Kings Cross; an old bloke who fixed pianos for a living; another whose local pub had been The Four in Hand in Darlinghurst for the past twenty years; interior designers who had been offering their services for as long as I had been alive; retired detectives from the homicide squad who recalled the case as if it had happened yesterday; Double Bay retailers; aging television personalities and Florence's son Robert whose hair (according to his wife Annie) went grey in the week following his mother's death.

The next thing I knew, Florence's world started to overlap mine. I met friends of friends who'd known her and even discovered that I had grown up in a house papered with her designs. After looking at *Belle* and *Vogue Living* magazines, which had featured my childhood home, I discovered the powder room was emblazoned with one of Florence's most complex wallpaper designs—Peacocks. The life-sized exotic birds were displayed on a metallic background and I remember staring up at the wallpaper as a child, counting the feathers and marvelling at the shimmering print designed in a wild array of coppers, silvers and earthy tones. Florence's wallpapers provided the perfect match to the rest of the home that my mother had lovingly decorated in high-seventies style: brown suede walls, mottled marble vanities, soft cedar panelling and Italian pendant lights.

A few years after starting my investigation, my journey turned into a pilgrimage. With my father and six-month-old daughter Evie I explored the Queensland cattle station where Florence was born, paid homage to Broadhurst family graves, dined in her family home and drove to Hervey Bay where her ancestors had arrived in the 1860s. Eventually I ended up at the North Ryde Crematorium in Sydney where I sprinkled rose petals on her memorial.

In June 1999 I had an article published on Florence in the *Sydney Morning Herald's* 'Good Weekend' magazine. Later the same year I penned a host of articles on Florence for *Vogue Living*, the *Australian, Marie Claire Lifestyle, Australian Style* and *Monument*. Very little had been published on her life and work since her murder in 1977 and many of her contemporaries had died. With such a character as Florence, separating legend (created by herself and others) from fact was a detective job in itself.

A life by design is the story of Florence Broadhurst's life and a legacy of her work.

Siobhan O'Brien
September 2004

MURDER

1977

'My success is the fact that my wallpapers have now
become a status symbol.'

FLORENCE BROADHURST, *PERSONALISATION PAYS OFF*, SPEECH 1976

$\mathcal{I}$t was just after the close of business on Saturday, 15 October 1977, when Florence Maud Broadhurst cast an eye over her studio-factory on Royalston Street in Sydney's Paddington. Since arriving at 8.45 am, the studio had been a hive of activity: employees washing print-screens, mixing paint, checking colours and drawing designs before printing them on the fourteen-metre-long tables that filled the lower level of the factory. The telephone had not stopped ringing throughout the day and a constant stream of clients added to the chaos—three of them were still rifling through the shelves bursting with 6000 designs in Florence's upstairs office. Most of her employees had left for the day, but her head printer, David Bond, and Albert Roberts, a cleaner and silk-screen printer, were wiping shelves and sweeping the ink-splattered floor. From nearby Trumper Park, children's cries could be heard as they kicked a football.

It had been one of Florence's typically savvy business decisions to move the factory to the fashionable Sydney suburb of Paddington from the more industrial Crows Nest. She could have done it sooner than 1969. Paddington was a cosmopolitan suburb and Florence felt more in touch there with 'her people' as she liked to call her clients, friends and acquaintances—those who were attracted to the heady world of art, design and fashion. Since the early sixties, Paddington had morphed into a hot-spot for middle-class Bohemians and left-wing idealists. It was multicultural, full of suburban escapees, with streets lined with boutiques, showrooms, galleries, wine bars and deli-catessens run by Greeks and Italians still doing brisk business late into the evening. Artists such as Margaret Olley, Donald Friend and Jeffrey Smart were also attracted to the buzz and culture of the area, while the Hungry Horse Gallery and Restaurant provided a venue for artists like Brett Whiteley, Robert Hughes, John Olsen, Robert Klippel and Clement Meadmore. Writers such as Mungo MacCallum, Cyril Pearl and Annette Macarthur-Onslow were also working behind the doors of smart thirties terrace houses, where fancy dress parties and partner swapping was the norm.

The façade of Florence's studio-factory didn't look much from the street. All that differentiated it from the brick terraces and factory buildings that surrounded it was a colourful awning with a scalloped edge that sat like a hood above the main front door. The design on the awning was printed by Nerida Greenwood, an employee of Florence's between 1967 and 1970, and featured large, bold flowers on a plain white background. On either side of the front door large black plaques read 'Florence Broadhurst. London–New York–Hawaii'. Underneath each of these plaques camellias that matched the colour of the building stood in large white pots. Other than these minor embellishments, the studio-factory was just a two-storey cement-block building with a saw-tooth roof. Inside, it was something else altogether.

•

Florence had come a long way in the twenty years since she set up her wallpaper business in 1959. Little did she know back then that designing, printing and producing custom-designed wallpaper would be so profitable and so fun. Not only was she now well established socially and financially, she had a loyal and influential clientele, she exported her wallpapers to London, New York, Hawaii, Paris, Kuwait, Madrid and Oslo, and had secured prestigious international commissions. According to fashion writer and former model Maggie Tabberer, '*Anyone* who was *anyone* decorated their homes with one of her designs.'

Even though the 'indefatigable Churchillian dynamo', as her ex-husband Leonard Lloyd Lewis called her, was seventy-eight years old by this time, she still walked to work every morning from her nearby home at Belgravia Gardens, Darling Point. And when she wasn't walking, she was catching taxis to a relentless round of charity and social functions. Leslie Walford, an interior designer who knew Florence for twenty years, remembers her as 'a dynamic, determined character who worked very, very hard'. According to Florence, 'There is no substitute for hard work, whether you are an artist or in business . . . you must get down to an exacting schedule and fulfil your obligations. You have to work hard to be successful' (Thompson, 1971). As she noted in her diary while living in London in the thirties: 'The difference between stepping-stones and stumbling blocks is how you use them.'

Florence retained the bird-like beauty of her youth even into her late seventies. According to ex-husband Leonard in an interview in the *Australian Women's Weekly* in 1977, 'People disbelieved her age. She hoodwinked them for years. Most felt she was around eighteen years younger than she was. Few knew she was really seventy-eight.' But the vigour and healthy appearance was a mask for Florence's failing health. She was hard of hearing and nearly blind from the cataracts creeping over her eyes. Her inability to see well in her old age may have contributed to her passion for exaggerated colours—lime green, hot pink, bright sapphire blue, fluorescent yellow, gold, bronze and copper.

During the seventies Florence's natural good looks had been replaced with glitzy artifice. She now donned wigs, had facelifts, fluttered false eyelashes, pancaked her makeup and wore large gold earrings that, combined with strategically coiffed red hair, hid her hearing aids. Ex-employee Nerida Greenwood claims Florence often called on her workers to 'run repairs', which meant help her stick her eyelashes back on if they had come adrift or to rouge her cheeks where the makeup had rubbed off. Florence's sister Priscilla once remarked, 'If she has another facelift she won't have any eyebrows left.'

•

On Saturday, 15 October 1977, the morning of her murder, Florence had walked to work along her usual route past cafés, corner stores and newspaper stands as cars, buses and trams rattled past. She wore her usual pant-suit but with an unusually sedate cream blouse and black cardigan. She had entertained some clients in her showroom on the previous evening—one of her many spontaneous parties that were often favourably reported in the press.

When she arrived at the studio-factory she had a chat with David Bond and Albert Roberts, who were busy printing wallpaper on the lower level. About an hour later, Florence retreated to the upstairs showroom where she cleaned up, did some bookwork, made a few phone calls and waited for a barrage of clients.

According to David Bond, he and Albert Roberts had arrived at work, accompanied by an ex-employee, Richard Gill, at 6.20 am. Richard lingered in the studio-factory for a short time before he left. At midday David joined Richard at the nearby Four in Hand pub where the two friends had lunch. Shortly after 1 pm David returned to work. At 2 pm Florence asked him to prepare a sample for clients, who he described in his statement to police as 'a middle-aged Jewish couple with a bluey-silver coloured poodle'. When David finished preparing the sample, he took it upstairs where Florence waited with her clients. Florence allegedly mumbled that she did not want to waste any more time with the Jewish couple as she was hoping to 'get a good sale' from other clients, who were waiting for her attention nearby.

At 2.35 pm, David Bond and Albert Roberts changed out of their paint-splattered overalls into casual attire before they walked upstairs to collect their pay. According to David, it was customary for employees to be paid their weekly salary on Friday afternoon and 'any employee who is required to work on a Saturday gets paid in cash by Miss Broadhurst'. As the two weary workers waited for Florence at the entrance of the showroom, three customers—a solid man of five-foot ten-inches (about 178 centimetres) who wore a green short-sleeved shirt, his female companion, a brunette who wore her hair closely cropped and a woman in her late forties who wore a fashionable one-piece pant-suit—rifled through samples of wallpaper. When Florence spotted David, she allegedly said, 'This is my head printer. You'll have to excuse me as I have to pay him.' Florence then walked to her desk, produced a beige wallet from her large black handbag and handed the men their money. As David turned to leave he said to Florence, 'I know what I'm printing on Monday, so I have no worries.' Florence replied, 'You know what you're doing, David.'

After a long day at work, the two men sauntered over to the Whitehall Hotel on New South Head Road for a couple of beers. David claims he left the studio-factory directly after he received his pay, but his fellow employee allegedly returned to lock the two rear double doors. Albert later joined David at the hotel.

When the last of her clients left at approximately 3.30 pm, Florence went upstairs to the kitchenette, which was separated from the office and showroom by a curtain. It was a small space with a stainless-steel sink, electric stove, built-in cupboards, separate shower recess and a toilet with a hand basin. She opened the fridge and selected a carton of yoghurt, swallowing a few spoonfuls and nibbling on some segments of an orange, the uneaten segments of which she left on the sink. About ten minutes later, neighbour Wendy Soan, who lived at 27 Royalston Street, noticed Florence on the first floor, closing a window and pulling down the blinds. According to Wendy, 'I knew that it was Miss Broadhurst because I could see her bright red hair, and she was wearing a black jumper with long sleeves. It also led me to believe it was Miss Broadhurst as it was her usual duty or practice to close all the windows and blinds before she leaves.'

Even though Florence wore hearing aids, she was still hard of hearing. So, as she cleaned up her afternoon tea she had no idea that an intruder had snuck in under the awning and through the front door downstairs. As he walked past the printing tables that were a tangle of screens and paint pots, he picked up a piece of timber that was allegedly used to stir the pot of vinyl coating that Florence applied to her wallpaper. The timber was freshly sawn at one end. He climbed the stairs that led to Florence's office and confronted her in the kitchenette.

The fight was vicious. As Leonard, her ex-husband, explained in an interview that he gave to the *Australian Women's Weekly* shortly after her death, 'She was not one to be intimidated, and confronted by an intruder it would not be Florence's nature to be meek, but rather the opposite. Her determination may have contributed to her death.' Leslie Walford agreed, 'Her killer would have had a hard time, because Florence would've attacked them, verbally at least.'

Even though her spirit was strong, the elderly Florence was overpowered and in the struggle she dropped a tea towel and lost her dentures, both of her hearing aids and a gold earring. The intruder chased her to the washroom, then to the kitchenette, and finally back to the toilet adjacent the washroom. Florence sustained massive head injures. The intruder, who the police alleged bludgeoned Florence nine times in her face and once on the back of her head, fractured her sternum, broke her nose, the thyroid bone in her throat and the bone at the back of her right eye socket, then shoved her head into the toilet and pulled the chain. When found, Florence was in a seated position on the concrete floor. Her left leg was bent with the knee tucked up near the left shoulder and her right leg was outstretched on the floor. Her bloodied left cheek lay on the rim of the toilet bowl, near the broken seat. Plastic fragments of the toilet seat floated in the water. Her top dentures lay on the cistern, her bloodied mouth was slightly ajar. Her limp right arm flopped into the bowl that had been plugged with her cardigan and blouse and the rings that usually adorned her left hand were nowhere to be seen. Some of her red hair was pasted in wet streaks across her face and was caked with congealed blood, while the rest of it hung down into the toilet bowl. Mascara ran down her face. Her fingers had been crushed to a pulp. Fragments of bloodstained timber, a gold earring, a false eyelash and a segment of orange lay on the floor nearby. Another hearing aid lay between her legs. Two metres above Florence's body was an impression of the fabric of her pantsuit on the fibro wall of the toilet. The bloodied imprint suggested that her killer had either rammed or thrown her body with brutal force into the wall. On the opposite wall there was a blood-stained impression of her head.

Her killer knew his way around well enough to escape by the rear doors, which he had had to unlock to exit. He then placed bricks against the doors so they could not be pushed open from the inside, presumably in case Florence was still alive, thus preventing her from leaving the premises. With a key kept on a nail by the door jam, he unlocked a padlock holding a chain on the rear gate of the factory, locked the padlock from the outside and took the key with him.

At 4.15 pm Sue Christine McCarthy and her mother and sister pulled up in a red Fiat out the front of Florence Broadhurst Wallpapers on Royalston Street—they had hoped to buy some wallpaper that afternoon. The three women walked in through the front door that had been left ajar and climbed the stairs to the first floor. They waited for a few minutes and went downstairs to the lower level. They called out several times. There was no answer, so they returned to the first floor where they called out again. Sue walked into the kitchenette but the door to the washroom was closed. She knocked on the door, but everything was still and silent. She did not see a hearing aid lying on the floor nearby. At 4.30 pm, Sue and her family left. It is quite probable that the killer was hiding somewhere on the premises or had just left.

It was a murder that shocked Sydney's society set. As Maggie Tabberer recalled, 'Sydney felt like it had been run over by a steam train the morning we opened the papers and saw that Florence had died . . .'

•

Who murdered Florence Maud Broadhurst and exactly why is still a mystery, and so is her life. She lived a tangle of contradictions, inventions and half-truths. She kept her Queensland childhood a secret, claiming she was an Englishwoman, and acted out roles, as she did on stage. She yearned for an aristocratic background and wove an intricate web of lies to cover her working-class roots. But those roots would not be buried; some details kept resurfacing during her numerous entrepreneurial endeavours. In one lifetime she seemed to live many lives, appearing in her own real-life drama in a number of guises: Bobby Broadhurst, the Shanghai minx; Florence Kann, British royalty's best friend; Madame Pellier, couturier to the stars; and Florence Lloyd Lewis, the trucking baron's wife.

With her flamboyant clothes and perfectly coiffed and hennaed hair, Florence cut a dashing figure on the social scene throughout her life. A devoted fundraiser for charity, she was also a sought-after public speaker and hostess, but she was more than just a social butterfly.

Variously described as eccentric, vain, self-absorbed, sharp tongued and ostentatious, Florence was also regarded as generous, loving, spirited, fearless and loyal. She was socially gregarious, but avoided intimacy with friends; she had an astute business mind, but the whimsy of an artist; she gushed over her customers (they were called 'darling') and treated her workers with contempt (they were called 'fools'); she was an unapologetic snob but said her greatest ambition was to 'play marbles with wharfies'. While living in London during World War II, she wrote: 'I am interested in people not pedigrees—if I like the Joneses I don't care if they came over with the conqueror or have just arrived from the colonies.' But her actions rarely followed this philosopy.

John Lang, a one-time employee, described Florence as 'nervous yet lonely. What the public saw was a great, blazing, fierce, endearing redhead who rattled her bracelets at them.' Peter Leis, another employee, described his former boss as almost impossible to work for. He painted a picture of an eccentric woman who responded to flattery, but would talk to a kerosene heater 'as if it were a lover—referring to it as "beautiful" or "terrific". I was a bit frightened of her—most people were, but you could always sweet-talk her. If you paid her compliments about her hair or her hat you'd have her wrapped around your little finger.' Leis, who attended a number of work-related functions with his boss, also claimed that if she attended an event that she felt was 'beneath her', she would make remarks such as 'these aren't my people'.

Designer Leslie Walford used to drop in for a chat and to mix his own colours in Florence's studio: 'She was a red-hot character, a red-hot mama, bright-eyed and flame-haired. She was fierce and determined with sassy sex appeal . . . still having affairs into her seventies. But there were people around who were scared stiff of Florence Broadhurst.' Maggie Tabberer agreed she was sassy, but added: 'She looked mad with her incredible hair in cochineal pink. Today it wouldn't raise an eyebrow, but in those days it was simply alarming.' Leanne Whitehouse, the director of Whitehouse School of Design and

Fashion, claimed: 'In her day, Florence Broadhurst was God!'

Jeanette Mosely was the subject of a portrait painted by Florence in 1961. She provided an insight into Florence the artist. 'She was unapproachable, commanding and spoke with clipped, quick English tones through a stiff chin, lips and teeth. Her attitude was, "you have come to sit for me, now sit". She made me nervous, the way she looked me up and down, it made me feel creepy.'

Sally Fitzpatrick, who worked with Florence, said that the Florence she knew spoke at a million miles an hour in a mad gibberish, which was probably a result of her inability to hear as well as she once could. 'You'd say something to Flo, either in person, on the phone or in the studio, and she'd reply, "What? What? Who? Who? Oh, fabulous, fabulous darling." With Flo everything was always, "What? What? Who? Who?"'

A striking woman, despite her diminutive five-foot four inches (about 163 centimetres), Florence left an impression of being 'tall' and 'statuesque'. She had a fine-boned frame and her face was petite and heart-shaped, with a high, wide forehead and high cheekbones. Her chin was weak, small and pointed and she had unusual large, grey cat-like eyes that were alert, piercing and enquiring. According to Jeanette Mosely, Florence's eyes, accentuated with lashings of black kohl and mascara, darted with nervous energy. But, as Jeanette also said, less flatteringly, 'she was poppie eyed—like she had a thyroid problem'.

It was Florence's unusually luminous red hair that was her signature. She went through a temporary phase of dying it pink, while later she wore an elegant blonde French roll, but it didn't take long before she returned to her favoured fiery shade of red. Much to the dismay of her long-suffering hairdresser in the Sydney suburb of Edgecliff, Florence would often produce a lock of her own hair that she had kept from her childhood, and say 'colour me carrot!'

GROWING UP

1899–1922

'With the help of God, and with no other mortal ever
to know . . . I shall do great things.'

<small>FLORENCE MAUD BROADHURST, FIFTEEN YEARS OLD</small>

*I*t all started for Florence not, as she may have wished and as most probably thought, in some aristocratic Georgian mansion in England, but amongst the flies and dust of Mungy Station, a large cattle property on the outskirts of Mount Perry in north-west Queensland. There was no Shakespearian theatre or European boutiques for hundred of thousands of acres—just bush, rocks and scrub, cattle, dust and huts with corrugated-iron roofs. It was inside one of these huts, with blowflies buzzing about the meat safe, that Florence was born on 28 July 1899, or 26 August 1899, depending on whether you go by her birth certificate or her death certificate.

Only a year had passed since Florence's mother, Margaret Ann Broadhurst nee Crawford, had lost a daughter named Maude who had lived for just twelve days, one of five of her children lost in childbirth. Florence's first moments were watched by her three-year-old sister, May Millicent, and four-year-old brother, Fassifern, who peered up at their mother, who was propped up by pillows in her four-poster bed holding tiny Florence in her arms.

None of her family could have conceived of the life that lay before the little redhead who lay wailing and thrashing her legs.

•

By those days' standards Florence's family was close-knit and close by. Her grandparents on her father's side lived at Sharston Mount, a remote property 30 kilometres from Childers (located between Maryborough and Bundaberg), where they'd been for almost twenty years. Florence's grandfather, William Broadhurst, had taken a long time to put down roots. Sailing into Hervey Bay from Liverpool in 1865 with his wife, Elizabeth Broadhurst nee Johnson, aboard the optimistically named *Golden Land* had conjured up a mixture of feelings. The shoreline of 'the promised land' was a tangle of mangroves, palm trees, rocky outcrops and mud flats. The khaki shadows of the horizon and sea blended together and the eerie outline of Fraser Island rose up from the ocean like a shadowy giant. They had to wait nineteen days before they could set foot on the mainland because a fever had broken out on board the *Golden Land*. When a government steamer finally arrived to take them to the mainland it was too late for three of their fellow passengers. They were buried in the sand dunes of Woody Island.

Only a year after Florence's grandparents arrived in Queensland, Elizabeth was pregnant with John, the first of twelve children. Bill, Florence's father, was next. William worked for a while in a variety of jobs—at sawmills, dairy farms and such. Then, with a growing family to feed, he joined the hundreds of hopefuls in the Gympie Gold Rush in 1867 before settling in Kolbore, where he began dairying. On roads that were little more than bush tracks, he carted, once a week, butter, eggs and bacon the 33 undulating miles (about 53 kilometres) to Maryborough. It wasn't long before William's butter, according to the *Bundaberg Daily News and Mail* of the time, was 'in popular demand . . . on account of its unrivalled excellence'.

When Florence's father, William 'Bill' Broadhurst, and his new bride, Margaret, moved to Mount Perry in the late 1890s, a railway line had been installed from Bundaberg to Mount Perry. The newlyweds had been attracted to the picturesque township for more reasons than fertile soil, plentiful water and land grants. Copper and gold were discovered in Mount Perry in 1869 and the sleepy town, dominated by the verdant 750-metre peak by the same name, became a boom town overnight. By the time the couple arrived, after Bill had been granted land in the area—410 acres (approximately 166 hectares) at Kullogum and 873 acres (approximately 353 hectares) at Wolca—in July 1885, the town's success could be measured by its twenty-three hotels, five churches and a plethora of businesses: butcher shops, blacksmiths, cobblers, saddlers, storekeepers, dairies and cordial makers. Surrounding scrub farms produced pineapples, bananas, mangoes, peanuts and cotton. The area was also extremely good cattle country.

Rather than tending his own land, Bill decided to take a job as station manager for William Sly, the owner of Mungy Station. It was regarded as one of six biggest and best cattle stations in the area and at one time covered 300 000 acres (approximately 122 000 hectares). Located eighteen kilometres west of the township, beyond the rocky Normandy Range and steep Possum Creek Range, the property, which still exists, has two creeks running through it—Possum Creek and Reid's Creek. It is the latter that snakes through the rocky outcrops and willow trees near the cluster of huts that was Florence's birthplace.

Bill Broadhurst was a straight-talking larrikin renowned for his dry wit, great strength and relentless endurance. Ted Bettiens, who still lives in a yellow fibro house on the outskirts of Mount Perry, worked by his side on Mungy Station for almost a decade. Bill and Ted set out droving once a week and stayed out for up to five nights before returning home to their families on weekends. While most men would have found the constant separation from their loved ones lonely, it suited Bill's natural independence, fierce spirit and determination. Their days were filled with mustering and feeding cattle, tending lucerne crops, fixing fences and taking care of Bill's invaluable horses. At night they smoked rollies around a campfire until the early hours and, depending where they were, slept in hessian sacks slung between trees that they 'climbed into like a pair of possums'. According to Ted, the pair survived on tea, jam and bread that was so mouldy 'it needed shaving'. When Bill later became the wealthy owner of numerous properties in the local area, including a 9000-acre (3640-hectare) property called Elliott's Creek, he would joke that his side of the fence was 'the shiny side' and the neighbours owned 'the rusty side'.

In character, Bill's wife, Margaret, was his polar opposite. Naturally tentative, she was quietly spoken and reserved; a woman who 'clung to the house' according to locals. Reid's Creek was her saving grace. Just a stroll down the hill from the huts, it made life in the harsh conditions more bearable. Like Bill, Margaret was from a big family of twelve siblings, so she knew well the work involved in raising a brood. Born in Tenterfield, her mother, Jane Fletcher, moved to the Maryborough district in 1867, where she married Thomas Girvan Crawford on 31 January 1868. Thomas was a robust, energetic timber getter who was an itinerant worker in a variety of locations including Tin Can Bay, Nanango and Dunmora. It was when they were based at Dunmora that their daughter Margaret had married Bill Broadhurst on 9 October 1894 in a Methodist ceremony, followed by a modest country reception.

•

Cattle grazing was in Bill's blood but he was first and foremost a horseman. Between 1902 and 1904 he delivered mail between Mount Perry and Kariboe, a weekly five-day ride that tested even his toughened resolve. It is likely that Bill was lured by the job's steady annual salary of one hundred and forty-six pounds. The birth of his third daughter, Priscilla 'Cilla' Margaret, meant another mouth to feed.

With Bill's career change came a change of residence. In 1902, when Florence was three years old, the Broadhurst family left the cluster of huts at Mungy and shifted to a one-hundred-and-twelve-acre (five-hectare) property at Drummers Creek known as 'The Oakes'. The sizeable home, a mere five kilometres to the east of Mount Perry, was luxurious by comparison with Mungy Station. It had broad, sweeping verandas with stairs rising to a peak at the front of the building. The interiors boasted cedar finishes, high ceilings and spacious living areas. This building is no longer standing, but on the same property The Pines, which the family subsequently lived in from 1930–73, was built in 1871 and has been kept in immaculate order by its current owner, Pat Smith. The white colonial homestead features a dramatic curved corrugated-iron roof, wide verandahs, a formal dining room, polished floorboards throughout, theatrical velvet drapes, Spanish pendant lighting, an overgrown private tennis court (the only one in town), and a creek bed in close proximity. Pat is also the owner of a host of Broadhurst memorabilia: Bill's walking stick that features a silver handle in the shape of a bird's skull and his steel matlock (affectionately call 'Bill'), paintings by Florence, four-poster beds, dolls and furniture. Today, the home is surrounded by a glorious garden that is abundant with towering date palms, climbing roses, frangipanis and mulberry vines.

•

Living close to town at The Oakes was a novelty for Florence and her three siblings. From 1902 until 1915, Mount Perry experienced its second great boom. In 1907 the population soared to almost 4000, which made it approximately the same size as Cairns and Mackay and only slightly smaller than Bundaberg. On Saturday nights Margaret and Bill would wheel Priscilla around town in her pram, while Florence, May and Fassifern trotted alongside. They joined the miners and their families promenading the streets under the glow of oil and gaslights until 9 pm. Late-night shoppers crowded the counters of stores such as the Amos Brothers, where pieces of cod and ling hung from the ceiling like sides of bacon. Other businesses that had recently moved to town included an oyster saloon, a tobacconist, a baker, a café and a jewellery store. And there were now billiard tables at the Grand Hotel.

Florence reflected on this period in her life while living in London during World War II. She wrote: 'The secret of never growing old is never to have been bored in your youth. Looking back, I can see how lucky I was in that during the three formative years of my adolescence I went to a day school and was therefore thrown upon my own company for a long period every week. It incalculated in me the need for self-sufficiency, that little by little was met and finally strengthened.'

Florence developed a self-sufficiency that came not so much from her schooling but from how she was raised: to be independent, resourceful and make the most of what she had. She had to entertain herself with her own dreams and her own plans. While a number of children in the area either had tutors, were sent away to boarding school or weren't educated at all, school for Florence was a mere stroll across a paddock to the Mount Perry State School. Here Florence developed a wide variety of interests: she rode horses, tended vegetable and fruit gardens, cooked, painted, read, sewed, knitted, showed a formidable talent in music and singing and cultivated her passion for tennis inherited from her father, who was still serving and volleying in his eighties.

Florence was only eleven years old when in 1910 she joined the local Children's Tennis Club with her sisters. According to family friend Ted Bettiens, sport—including football, rifle shooting, horseracing, wood chopping and cricket—meant a lot to the Broadhursts who 'always got fired up about competition and about winning first prize'. Since early settlement, tennis played a pivotal role in the community, and by the early 1900s there were three public tennis clubs in Mount Perry.

When Florence and her sisters were older, they spent hours pinning their hair, painting their faces and fitting their frocks for the Race Ball that, since 1872, was a high point on the Mount Perry social calendar. From far-flung locales around the district, young men and women flocked to town to dance to the double bass, drums, accordion and guitar that played until the wee hours at the

Patterson's Royal Hotel or the Victoria Hotel. At other times of the year they gathered at the Federal Hall to dance to visiting brass and pipe bands. On one such occasion, Florence's brother Fassifern played a trick on a gaggle of unsuspecting women. Disguised as a ghost with a sheet over his head, he hid by a creek and pounced on them as they walked past.

Unlike his self-sufficient sisters 'who were as clever as anyone in the bush', Fassifern developed a reputation as a shady character and in 1919 he was arrested on a charge of stealing sixteen head of cattle from the owner of Mungy Station. Ted Bettiens reckons Fassifern had picked up some of his tricks from Bill, who on occasion falsified the age of his stock for better returns. As Ted explained, 'Bill would heat up a piece of wire and re-brand his herd, and when he was accused of it, he'd say, "But I have a witness, Bettiens was with me", to which I would reply, "Yes, I was there when they branded—both times".'

Florence's sister May, on the other hand, had a temperament like her mother's. She rarely ventured out but showed her father's skill in the saddle. That was probably all she inherited from him. Florence and Priscilla were both like Bill. Cilla was an outgoing, colourful character who was the life of parties, played the piano like a professional and, according to locals, 'drank most people under the table'. Contemporaries remember Florence as a fiercely determined child, with a raucous laugh, tons of grit, a memory like an elephant, wild red hair and an inquisitive nature. She was passionate about the arts, and her eyes lit up when the travelling picture showman came to town to show his flickering silent black-and-white films, or when amateur theatricals, musicals and debates featured at the School of the Arts. From an early age she spent her days listening to Gladys Moncrieff—'Australia's Queen of Musical Comedy'—on the gramophone and dreamed of following in her footsteps. It didn't take long for the naturally ambitious Florence to understand that her fine contralto voice may be her ticket out of the life of Mount Perry.

THE ORIENT

1922–1927

'Both Europeans and Americans love China, because
it is so completely flattering to the Anglo-Saxon sense of
racial superiority'

VOGUE, 1924

When Florence was fifteen years old she wrote an enlightening manifesto entitled 'Resolution'. It contains surprisingly well-formed ideas for someone so young and reveals her raw ambition:

I shall do great things. My name shall not be lauded but in my way I shall do great things. I shall not let personal ambition and greed grip my soul in its hungry hands. I will not let my youth slip away without laughter and the joy of living making my face bright and my will strong. I will not be evil; neither shall I speak of evil to others. I will not judge, for no man is worthy enough to judge his neighbour. I will grasp the goodness and the beauty of life, and throw away the ugliness and bitterness. I will turn my face to the light; yet remember the darkness that lies behind and around me. I will not blame others for my many sorrows and defeats, for man has but himself to blame for failure. Yes, I will fail and in failing I will try again. I will fall and in falling, climb. Yes, I will be selfish, for ultimately I will gratify and bring happiness to myself by giving it away in large measures to others . . . No real happiness can come to him who keeps his happiness to himself and does not share it with the whole world. Sympathy, sorrow, joy, yes, even anger will be my lot and I will thank God that I have the depth to feel all these things. I will thank Him for the glorious beauty of the world at sunset, for the unbearable sweetness of song. For the million, million things which lie in wait for us every hour of the day, to please our sight and fill our eyes with perfection. And I shall envy no man, for the things which are precious and everlasting can be found in our own heart. Yes, with the help of God, and with no other mortal ever to know . . . I shall do great things.

At about the same time as Florence wrote this manifesto, she turned up for her first singing lessons with Kate Gratehead, a charitable woman who organised a host of musical events during World War I to raise money for Australian servicemen abroad. Florence was a dedicated student. Once a week, May hitched up her horse and buggy and took her younger sister to the Mount Perry Railway Station, where Florence caught the train to Bundaberg. Kate Gratehead was able to fine-tune the budding contralto, and Florence soon scooped up a clutch of awards at eisteddfods in Bundaberg and Toowomba. The *Bundaberg Daily News and Mail* described Florence as a 'promising contralto' whose 'fine singing at the 1918 Eisteddford is not likely to be forgotten . . . she sang splendidly, her beautiful contralto voice with a fine range . . . delighted the audience who insisted on her reappearing when she was presented with a bouquet . . .'

Florence's song of choice for the eisteddford—advertised in the local newspaper as a 'Grand Concert – Queen's Theatre. Proceeds in Aid of Patriotic fund. God Save the King'—was 'Still as the Night' composed by Georg Bohm.

Florence's single-minded determination soon paid off. At sixteen she won a prize to perform a duet with a famous English contralto named Dame Clara Butt, who is still considered one of the greatest voices of the first three decades of the twentieth century. Dame Clara toured the world, giving concert performances of ballads and oratorios. She first fell in love with Australia in 1907 and continued to travel here until ill health prevented her. When she discussed her 1907 program with the Australian diva Dame Nellie Melba, she was famously advised to 'sing 'em muck it's all they understand'. By all accounts Dame Clara paid Dame Nellie no heed. Together Florence and Clara sang 'Abide with Me', a rendition that threatened to lift the roof of the Brisbane Anglican Cathedral. In later life Florence described this moment as the pinnacle of her singing career.

But there was more to come. When Florence was in her early twenties she auditioned for a musical comedy troupe known as the Smart Set Diggers, who did a number of seasons at the Princess Theatre in Toowoomba, the Empire in Brisbane and the Playhouse in Sydney. The hard working troupe was mostly made up of men who dressed up as women. They performed a melange of acts, including comedy routines, songs, short plays and piano recitals. The Smart Set Diggers had been captivating audiences since World War I when, under the management of Charles Holt, they had successfully entertained troops with their spicy antics.

Drag shows in army camps was a trend that began around 1915 and continued to flourish during the interwar period. They were frequently performed in hastily erected theatres, ruined cathedrals, tents, chateaux, huts and on open-air platforms to raise funds, put an end to the monotony of war or 'boost' troop morale. The performances featured male soldiers in crude makeup, makeshift wigs and frivolous frocks, ranging from racy strip teases to impersonations of movie actresses, chorus girls and other sexy starlets. The audiences that frequented these shows regarded them as vaguely naughty, humorous and not strictly homosexual—merely a routine that flirted with the idea of transgender. In 1942, the official photo caption for 'This Is the Army', a Broadway musical that toured the world and was eventually made into a movie, summed up the sentiment: 'Don't let them fool you, boys. They're chorus "gals" but tough as mule meat.'

On 27 December 1920, the Smart Set Diggers commenced a season at the Playhouse Theatre in Sydney. The following day a reporter from the *Sydney Morning Herald* reported that 'Four of the company gave an unexpectedly clever female impersonation. These were Charles Holt, Ralph Sawyer, "Tiki" Carpenter and Bobby Roberts.' A successful Sydney season was followed by performances at Brisbane's Empire Theatre. On 28 January 1921, *The Australia Variety and Show World* reported, 'The Smart Set Diggers made their first appearance at the Empire on Saturday and were greeted with a crowded house at both sessions. Most of the boys are clever in their work, and should have a successful season...Reg McLaughlin and Ralph Sawyer were successful in their "Des Apache" dance.'

At some point between March 1921 and December 1922, Florence Broadhurst joined the all-male cast of returned soldiers now based in Toowoomba. Her colleagues included ex-Gallipoli stretcher bearer Ralph Sawyer, ex-soldier Wallingford Tate, cross-dresser extraordinaire Charles Holt, Lindsay Kemble and Richard 'Dick' Norton, men with whom Florence would forge lasting friendships.

Dick Norton was also the entrepreneurial mastermind behind a theatrical musical and comedy company called the Globetrotters, which was based in Shanghai. He offered Florence a starring role in the company's show. Lured by the excitement of life in a foreign country, she accepted and, on 4 December 1922, at twenty-three years of age, Florence boarded a ship in Brisbane bound for China. Three of her new friends—Wallingford Tate, Dick Norton and Charles Holt—were also on board.

•

No world cruise at the time was complete without a stop in Shanghai. It was Asia's most cosmopolitan destination and a city with many faces. Inner-city streets were a tangle of rickshaws, cars, trams and cyclists dodging businessmen in smart suits, women with boyish bob haircuts, sailors on shore leave, wharfies, street hawkers and itinerants who carted their wares across their shoulders in back-breaking baskets. Opium dens, prostitution, gambling, extortion and violence were just part of the scenery. Living a highly privileged existence alongside all this was a large enclave of British, French, American and Japanese expatriates. Russians also lived in Shanghai but they had arrived under different circumstances—as refugees.

Shanghai was a city where foreign business and trade flourished. In the heart of the city, an acre of land cost up to one hundred and forty thousand pounds more than comparable land in the heart of London. On the fringes of the city's industrial areas and foreign settlements were countless shantytowns filled with filthy straw huts, where beggars searched for sustenance and children worked fourteen-hour shifts. As the French consul-general pointed out in 1924, 'Shanghai, which is a city of luxury, ought to think much more about the misery which is so common there.' Not even the fancy architectural influences from Norway to Italy could hide the poverty and squalor, nor the relentless influx of immigrants.

When foreigners moved to Shanghai, they tended to leave some of their constraints and conventions at home. On her arrival in this maelstrom, so different to Mount Perry, Florence likewise faced a choice: to reinvent herself, or fade into the background. She chose to morph into the semi-androgynous 'Bobby Broadhurst'—a singing, dancing coquette in a flapper dress (known as a Parisian garconne frock), sporting a highly styled red bob known as 'a shingle' and kohl-rimmed eyes. Florence would have been an attractive, young and confident foreigner who not only had the right attitude and mixed with the right crowd, but who courted the attention that entertainers such as herself received from the press. She appeared with great frequency in the *Shanghai Sunday Times*, the *China Press* and the *Shanghai Ladies Journal*. Gone was the tennis-playing teenager and in her place was a sophisticated, sexy vamp with a nom de guerre to match. 'Bobby' found her niche among the cultural elite—actors, writers, painters, musicians, dancers and singers—that made up part of the foreign expatriate population that had poured into the city since the late nineteenth century. And like many events in Florence's life, Bobby's timing was perfect.

•

Western-style dancing such as ballroom and jazz took Chinese society by storm after World War I and by the twenties dance and cabaret culture had become intrinsically linked with Shanghai itself, which by now had earned the nickname 'Le Paris de L'Orient'. Tea dances, charity balls, professional song-and-dance troupes (called *gewu-tuan*), ballet, dancing schools and social gatherings for student associations, government, military and professional organisations were all the rage—but it was cabarets that had the greatest impact on the Shanghai elite. An English journalist writing in 1927 observed: 'Nowhere in the world, I should think, are there so many cabarets in proportion to the total white population. They range from the cheap and respectable palais de danse to more select resorts with exotic names like 'Paradise', where beautifully dressed professional dancers obligingly dance with all comers on the sole condition they order champagne' (Field, 1999).

When Florence became 'Bobby' she cast aside her Australian past. Bobby, she decided, would be British. As one reviewer in the *Malay Mail*, on 17 February 1923, confirmed: 'Miss Bobby Broadhurst . . . has a well-trained voice and pronounces her words beautifully, a talent only too rare among English singers.' At the time pretending to be British was not uncommon, but what was uncommon was how far Florence went with the deception. Not only did she sign up as an active member of the British Women's Association, whose agenda was to replicate British home life in Shanghai, but she maintained that she was British for the next fifty years. When she was back living in Sydney from 1949 onwards, reviews in the *Australian Women's Weekly*, the *Sunday Telegraph*, the *Australian Magazine* and other periodicals regularly described her as 'an Englishwoman who came to Australia' and Florence did nothing to dispel the untruth. In fact she courted it. Asked why, Leslie Walford, who knew Florence for twenty years, put it succinctly: 'No one wants to be trailer trash.'

Milly Bennett, an American expatriate who lived in Shanghai in the twenties, described the way Western women at the time would anglicise themselves. 'It is appalling what can happen to the average . . . housewife when she gets within hailing distance of what she thinks is high society, especially if it happens to have a British accent . . . It made my flesh crawl to hear . . . women go around imitating the la-de-da manners of the British, "cheerioing" one another and imitating what was obviously a lower-class British accent although they did not know it, and filling up their heads with imperialistic nonsense' (Clifford, 1990).

In the Shanghai of the twenties expatriates made up eighty-five per cent of the city's population. In many senses Shanghai became their town, with the locals existing to serve them. The general view of the expats, who usually came with a team of servants, was summed up in *Vogue* in 1924: 'Both Europeans and Americans love China, because it is so completely flattering to the Anglo-Saxon sense of racial superiority . . . one accepts all the Chinese, dun coloured and inert, without personality, as a background for the white "foreigners" who are high spots of colour in the parade dominating the street crowd just as the small foreign population dominates and colours the life of the city' (Clifford, 1990).

Despite her pretensions, Bobby's onstage antics received rave reviews in publications such as the *Statesman*, 15 June 1923, which described her as having an 'arresting style and rich expressive voice, [that] was particularly captivating'. Another publication claimed she and the Globetrotters received rapturous applause after their fusion of cabaret, pantomime, cross-dressing and 'highly spicy' comedy (*Manchuria Daily News*, 1924), while advertisements in local newspapers and on billboards read, 'The Globetrotters. Mirth–Music–Melody–Comedy & Burlesque. Some of everything and everything of the best. Popular pre-war prices'. The troupe, which had between six and nine members (depending on which review you read), consisted of Bobby, Wallingford Tate, Dick Norton, Dick Crichton, Kitty Farrell, Leila Forbes, Dorothy Drew, Charles Holt and Ralph Sawyer. Each member had a unique role: Dick Norton was the master of ceremonies, Dick Crichton was a comedian, Wallingford was the accompanying pianist, Charles and Ralph were the titillating crossdressers (Ralph also had a dual role as a female impersonator and dancer), while Bobby enthralled the audience with her velvety voice.

Together the troupe travelled extensively to perform at theatres in India, Assam, Burma, Siam, the Malay States, Java, Sumatra and Japan, appearing at venues such as the Palace Theatre in Karachi; the Theatre Royal in Kowloon and the Royal Bangkok Sports Club, where they performed for the rich, the famous and the upper echelons of society. According to Florence, the King of Siam was present at one of their performances. Favourable reviews abounded: the *Peking Daily News* claimed they were 'the finest combination now touring the East'. The *Penang Gazette* and *Straits Chronicle* hailed them as '. . . clever, witty, musical and above all original . . .', while the *North China Star* enthused that 'not a dull moment passed from the time the curtain rose until it dropped again to close one of the most interesting evening's entertainments offered in Hong Kong for many a long month'.

A single image in the *Manchuria Daily News* captures the troupe's style: headbands, flapper dresses, swinging beads and pointed character shoes for the girls; dinner suits, starched white shirts, bow ties and slick oiled hair for the boys. But this particular publicity shot did not reveal the racy costumes and characters that Florence and the rest of the crew assumed on stage. Florence shimmied in a headdress with spikes that jutted out like horns and white feathers that splayed in a peacock fan above her head. Some of her costumes were a beaded figure-hugging frock that featured a feather boa collar and a feathered hemline; a Manto de Manila, or Cantonese shawl, which she wore as a dress; a skirt cut mid thigh, with a matching crop top, headband, sandals and Hellenic-inspired detailing; a baggy clown suit with a ruffled neckline and pom-poms; and a long, black cape that hid a sexy, strappy dress with cut away sleeves and layers of finely woven fabric. The makeup and hairstyles that she wore on stage were changed to suit each character—when she dressed like a diva she rimmed her eyes with kohl and wore a sharp bob; when she dressed like a clown her hair was pinned back and her face pancaked white with an exaggerated red mouth.

The troupe took days, sometimes weeks, to reach their ports of call. They often travelled long distances across oceans and along rivers and canals before they reached the theatre where they were scheduled to perform. When they arrived local employees helped them with their luggage, which included the stage sets, while the troupe made their way to their accommodation either by horse and cart, or in a car (if one was available). Barry Little claims that Florence told him and his wife, entertainer Jeannie Little, that '[Florence] had always dreamt of going to Asia to have a bearer and that's exactly what she had when she went on tour.'

Touring was a lengthy and gruelling process, but it was worth it. Florence had never seen such exotic land-scapes, streetscapes, faces or buildings: the streets of Japan were lined with Buddhist temples, Shinto shrines and blossom trees; the fields and terraced hills of Java were an elaborate network of canals, dams and aqueducts; and the Sumatran waterways were overloaded with boats, Dutch immigrants and produce such as rubber, tobacco and tea. It is probable that when the troupe didn't have to rehearse or perform they wandered through the local craft markets bartering with locals or took short boat trips to nearby villages. In Calcutta they would have wandered through narrow streets, endured the summer monsoons and admired Hindu dancers. While in Peking they would have marvelled at shops filled with jade and ivory sculpture and explored the Forbidden City.

Sometimes Florence went on day trips on her own: she trekked over the heavily guarded Khyber Pass from India into Afghanistan; traversed the Great Wall of China; visited the Taj Mahal with its chequered marble floor and Quran verses that dance around the building's archways; and went camel riding. According to Barry Little, 'There wasn't much Florence didn't do when she was over there. She visited opium dens, the lot—you name it she did it. She had a wild, wild time and when she talked about it, she had a twinkle in her eye.'

Though during her time there Florence absorbed aspects of (and learnt from) the myriad of cultures throughout the east, she seemed not to understand the true nature of these cultures. After all, it was the British colonial perspective that appealed to her most. As she told a reporter for the *Bundaberg Daily News and Mail* in 1927, 'It is wonderful how the British have made their authority respected in India. The British dominance in

India is positively thrilling. I knew a ruler of an independent Indian state—he had 70 wives, by the way—who dared not cross the border because the British resident said to him, "Keep in your own territory!" That is the sort of thing that you meet in India, that makes you feel proud that as an Australian, you are a Britisher.'

By early 1924 Florence and Wallingford Tate were concocting plans of their own. Together they abandoned the Globetrotters and formed half a musical-comedy quartet known as The Broadcasters. Jack Crighton and singer Beryl Lucina completed the circle. After a successful soiree at the Tent Hotel in Yokohama, Japan, the *Kobe Herald* claimed the Broadcasters were 'up to New York and London standards' and another reviewer declared, 'Miss Bobby's charming voice evoked enthusiastic encore calls.'

When The Broadcasters weren't on lengthy tours they were based in Shanghai performing at venues that included the Star Theatre, the French Club and the Carlton Club. In between gigs with her famous travelling troupes, Florence joined groups affiliated with the Carlton Club, including the Carlton Follies and the Carlton Sparklers. A popular venue on the Shanghai night scene, the Carlton attracted an elite crowd who crammed into the stylish building on most nights of the week for a glittering display of razzle-dazzle and goodtime girls.

An evening at the Carlton was a dusk-til-dawn affair. As one reporter working in Shanghai in the twenties wrote: 'Boozing went on excessively and ceaselessly, pick-me-ups in the morning, heavy, boozy Tiffin's and cocktail parties, teas, receptions and late dinners, and the whole, long night of drinking, dancing, carousing, stretching ahead of it. Few flesh and blood men could resist it. Few did' (Clifford, 1990). An American journalist recorded his thoughts more succinctly: 'When, if ever the sun did set for foreigners in Shanghai, it would go down to the popping of champagne corks' (Clifford, 1990).

The Carlton had its own movie house, a ballroom and an in-house orchestra. Ornate imitation rococo designs adorned the building's ceilings and walls, while on the fringe of the sizeable dance floor, chairs and tables were set with crisp linen tablecloths that fell to the floor and flowers cascaded over the edge of upstairs balconies. The Carlton's signature was a massive glass-domed ceiling in the ballroom through which you could see the stars.

However, there was another, darker, side of the Carlton. While the cabaret girls were shimmying across the stage in their skimpy outfits, the roof garden hosted boxing matches bloody enough to bring down the 'wrath of the Municipal Council' (Clifford, 1990); while a spot known as 'Blood Alley' was within spitting distance of the club.

•

Was Florence doing more with Wallingford Tate than drinking champagne? In photos from this period the pair appear together everywhere: on board a ship from Australia to the east, on weekends away with friends, in press photos larking about in their stage costumes. In a photo taken in a garden on one of their many adventures, Wallingford stands with another couple as Florence sits cross-legged on the ground at their feet. She is cradling a white cat and her dark eyes glare up at the photographer like two black pools. Wallingford was not an unattractive man. He was tall—around six-foot-two (about 188 centimetres)—with large eyes, large hands, a thick chest and an expressive face with a forehead that was broad and lined. He looked protective, masculine and sincere standing near Florence in this photograph. When he smiled his face lit up. When he didn't he looked serious and pensive. And though Florence had a big personality, she looked demure and almost school-girlish beside him.

Florence was doubtless fond of Wallingford (she kept a copy of his obituary among her personal papers decades later) but she probably only ever saw her relationship with him as a passing affair. They had fun together and, living in a foreign country, they weren't answerable to anyone but themselves. Florence knew her sojourn in the east was a stepping-stone in an adventurous life that would reach far beyond the Shanghai dance halls and opium dens. Though she probably found it glamorous that her boyfriend was a performer with whom she travelled to exotic places, Wallingford didn't aspire to much beyond what he was currently doing. He didn't make much money, had no real social standing and no burning ambition. And he knew Florence as the person she truly was: the girl from Mount Perry who had once performed with him in the Towoomba Smart Set Diggers. Deep down she yearned for more in a partner and much more out of life. But she was happy to have fun in the meantime.

The only correspondence that exists between Wallingford and Florence is from 15 December 1925, when 'Wally' sent Florence a telegram via the Eastern Extension Australasian & China Telegraph Company which read:

BOMBAY LCO BROADHURST CHARTERED BANK SHANGHAI. DEAREST [the following word has been scribbled out with pencil] FRIGTHFULLY [sic] WORRIED CABLE CONDITION IMMEDIATELY. ALSO SOONEST YOU CAN COME JOIN MUSICAL COMEDY LOVE WALLY EXCELSIOR BOMBAY.

One might wonder whether Florence was having Wallingford's child. Certainly she felt the telegram was important enough to keep among her personal papers. But Florence had her eyes on a bigger prize than marriage or fame.

Since arriving in Le Paris de L'Orient, she had been sharpening her entrepreneurial talons and, three years after her arrival (when she was twenty-seven years old), she opened the impressively named 'Broadhurst Academy Incorporated School of the Arts'—abbreviated locally to 'The Broadhurst Academy'. Her life with the Broadcasters (and to a large extent with Wallingford) was now over. The school's location, on the corner of Nanking Road (Shanghai's answer to New York's Fifth Avenue) and Kiangse Road (a renowned red light district), had a strange duality. Like the Carlton Club, it embraced two worlds. Nanking Road was lined with sky-high department stores, theatres, hotels, fur stores, silk stores and skating rinks, and Kiangse Road was filled with brothels, filth and squalor. Nanking Road represented the new China, while Kiangse Road embodied the old.

Shortly after the school opened on 15 February 1926, advertisements appeared in the *Shanghai Ladies Journal* and in the program for Shanghai's Lyceum Theatre. The ads said that the school was founded to 'provide expert tuition in every branch of Music and Elocutionary Studies, Journalism, Languages, Short Story Writing, Drawing, Painting, Pen Painting, Modern Ball-Room and Classical Dancing, Physical Culture'.

Florence handled the day-to-day affairs of her new business venture such as keeping the books, hiring employees and recruiting pupils, but she also provided tuition in 'voice production' that incorporated stage technique, public speaking, deportment and dramatic art classes. She offered banjolele (a cross between a ukulele and a banjo) tuition with an advertising hook that 'guaranteed' pupils could 'learn the banjolele in six lessons'.

There exists a black-and-white image of Florence taken shortly after she opened her school. She's wearing a flowing frock and swinging beads and looking out from under an upturned hat as she holds a banjolele in her lap. Her penetrating gaze seems to look far beyond the photographer. The photo appeared in the *Sunday Pictorial Section* of the *China Press* captioned 'Banjolele Wielder'.

The credibility of the Broadhurst Academy was enhanced by four associates who joined Florence in the well-appointed practise rooms. They included Daniel Melza, a famous and highly regarded violinist; Professor Kournitz Boulueva, a buxom Russian pianist who earned her stripes at the Dresden Conservatory of Music and whose role at the Broadhurst Academy was to 'prepare pupils for the Royal Academy of Music and London Trinity College'; Madame Boulueva (perhaps a relative of the buxom Russian) who taught classical dancing including 'Ballet, Simultaneous, Sensational, Acrobatic, Eccentric,

Buck, Soft Shoe, Toe Dancing' and physical culture classes that claimed to include 'scientific reducing exercises for stout figures'.

Offering classes of a more literary kind was Jean Armstrong who taught short story writing, advertising, languages, copywriting and journalism; while other teachers took classes in modern ballroom dancing, such as the novelty waltz, polo trot, tango blues, Charleston and jazz fox trot. As the academy became more established these teachers were joined by other tutors including Jacob Lihnos who, according to an article in the *Sunday Times*, was a 'noted artist who exhibited paintings . . . in England, Rome and Japan' and had 'recently arrived in Shanghai after a world tour'; Miss Gravitzki, a lyric soprano who taught voice culture; and Simons Bryan, the former conductor of the Moscow Opera, who launched an operatic and piano studio at the school.

The way in which Florence went about establishing her academy reveals that even at twenty-seven she was a shrewd businesswoman who had a firm handle on 'networking' and 'marketing' before the terms were even invented. Selling herself and her skills was a talent that seemed to come naturally. In a strategy designed to attract fee-paying students to her ever-expanding studio, she promoted her school on local Shanghai radio stations and hosted dancing demonstrations at the academy and in nightspots around the city. In mid July 1926 she performed a banjolele duet with one of her male students on the airwaves. A few months later she displayed her considerable dancing expertise with an assistant known only as 'Mr Gleron'. A *China Press* article from 3 October 1926 reads: 'Miss Broadhurst with her assistant instructor, Mr Gleron, as partner, delightfully demonstrated the attractions of the Valencia, Sevilla, Barcelona and the New Charleston. These are the dances that are expected to be all the rage during the coming season. The music for the first three named dances is particularly seductive and this, combined with the grace and perfect unison with which the couple moved, left little to be desired.'

As always, not everyone found the latest dance craze so agreeable. A local teacher of the tango penned a letter to the editor of the *North China Daily News*: 'The tango is the most beautiful dance, and beautiful things never die. And who is dancing the Charleston? No one except a couple of youngsters who like to show off for the amusement of onlookers. The Charleston will never become fashionable in Shanghai because everyone is afraid to appear ridiculous.' In a letter of response that can only be described as hyperbolic, Florence defended her dance of choice: 'Who can resist the bright strains of the Charleston?' she wrote. 'I contend that when people dance for enjoyment they will dance those dances that create the greatest joy. Hence, a tango for enjoyment, a Charleston for fun . . . Certainly it will not last for ever—everything must give way to fashion's fancies, and Shanghai, though removed from the world's centre, is not going to allow a craze to pass unhonoured—when London and New York Charleston, Shanghai will not be found wanting. And when the Royalty of England and the leading society of America give their patronage to a dance, be it Charleston, Blues or camel walk, Shanghai's small voice of protest will go unheard, while those who care will find the correct solution and join in the craze of the world. I am, etc. B. BROADHURST.'

•

By 1925, much as they tried to ignore it, Shanghai's golden years were waning and resident Westerners had little understanding of what was taking place or didn't want to know. In urban and rural China, members of the working class, students and intellectuals had started to speak out about foreign imperialistic ventures. In 1922, when agreements signed by the United Kingdom, United States and Japan at the Washington Conference failed to satisfy Chinese demands, boycotts of foreign-owned goods and imports had been instituted. In 1924 a short, violent struggle erupted between Jiangsu and Zhejiang militarists: it was a conflict that resulted in thousands of casualties.

Six thousand refugees from rural areas in China were pouring into Shanghai every day. By the end of September there were half a million in the city resulting in a dramatic shortage of jobs, food and places to live. Then, on 30 May 1925, when foreign gunfire shot down a crowd of demonstrators on Nanking Road, there was a furious response. It marked the beginning of a national revolution: the shedding of the old structure of foreign domination and the birth of radical anti-imperialist nationalism. The straight-talking rebel Sun Yat-Sen, who died in 1925, summed up the mood among many Chinese: 'I want to tell foreigners this: Shanghai is China—foreigners are guests here, we are the hosts, and if this fact is not realised, we shall have to take drastic measures' (Clifford, 1990).

Amazingly, through all of this, Florence and her performing arts peers were still a going concern. When a British division of 12 000 men, commanded by Major General John Duncan, set sail for China in January 1927— with the task of defending British Nationals in Shanghai—Florence was responsible for entertaining the troops with a band of artists calling themselves the Frothblowers. On 24 May 1927, she performed at the Lyceum Theatre for Empire Day where the bands from the defence force also played. As Florence said in an interview she gave on returning to Australia, 'There is no doubt, that the timely arrival of British troops at Shanghai saved the situation as far as foreigners in China were concerned.'

But there was more to come. In March 1927, Nationalist armies took control of Shanghai and Nanking. A strike led by communists in Shanghai aroused fears that the Chinese might seize the International Settlement, now barricaded with barbed wire and machine guns and guarded by a large international force. And on 12 April, in a bloody and brutal showdown, thousands of communists were executed by Nationalist troops.

The end of Shanghai's golden age captured world headlines and by July 1927 Florence had had enough. She left the memories of Wallingford Tate to the dance halls and clubs of Asia; she left the Broadhurst Academy in the hands of associates, and returned back home to Australia.

When Florence left, Wallingford knew he wanted to make a change. He did not want to return home to Australia so he did a stint with the Bandman Theatrical Company, touring through countries such as Gibraltar, Egypt, Ceylon and India. Later, he was with the army and did repatriation work during World War II. It didn't take long, however, before he returned to his first love—performing. He toured the east with the London Comedy Company and while travelling with this company in India Wallingford contracted typhoid and passed away. His obituary read:

Mr Wallingford Tate dead. Simla, 26th July.

The London Comedy Company, which is playing before crowded houses in Simla has sustained a severe loss in the untimely death of Mr Wallingford Tate at the age of 39. Mr Tate was seriously ill with enteric fever when the company were in Ootacamund. He left hospital three weeks ago. On Saturday evening he became ill and an operation was immediately performed. He died on Sunday evening. For many years he travelled the East and at one time was a prominent figure in the Bandman Company. During the war he served in Hodson's House. The funeral took place in Simla this afternoon, a large gathering being present, among which were officers of the deceased's late regiment.

When Florence returned to Australia, she described China in an interview with the *Bundaberg Daily News and Mail* as simply 'a country seething with bloodshed and tumultuous discontent'.

RETURN HOME

1927

'Florence Broadhurst is a woman who tossed the dice of fate in those far-flung lands across the watery plains.'

BUNDABERG DAILY NEWS AND MAIL, JULY 1927

$\mathcal{A}$ local scribe from the *Bundaberg Daily News and Mail* accosted Florence the moment she stepped from the Brisbane mail train onto the Mount Perry platform for the glamorous redhead was now famous. She had travelled, she had been successful and she had returned.

For an Australian woman to be newsworthy in the twenties she had to either get married, have a baby, organise a charity event or die—and even then these so-called milestones would only be written into her obituary. 'Ladies' interests' columns in newspapers sought to teach women what to cook (from cauliflower fritters to apple batter pudding and rainbow cakes) and what to wear (fur neck muffs, boneless girdles and blonde court shoes), kept them well versed on the art of etiquette ('don't fall into the old mistake that it's good to keep him waiting') and

all things bridal ('the floral scheme is hardly less important than the frocks').

Unlike her apron-strung contemporaries, the article
about Florence when she returned home from abroad
filled an entire page of the *Bundaberg Daily News and
Mail*. It described her grandiosely as a woman who had
'tossed the dice of fate in those far-flung lands across the
watery plains'. In the article, Florence voiced her opinions on everything from irrigation methods in Java,
whisky-soaked missionaries trying in vain to save souls,
and Chinese riots, to the caste system in India and the
'peculiar characteristics of the yellow races'. Her escapades
were described as 'a harvest of experiences, some of which
were not untinged with danger, most, for a great part,
capable of arousing in her listeners feelings, perhaps of
envy, certainly of considerable romantic interest'.

We know that Florence got more out of her travels than
a girls-own-adventure to tell the local newspaper. Her
four-and-half years in the orient would emerge not only
in her wallpaper designs and her artwork, but would
impact on her fashion-sense and personal style.

When she launched her wallpaper venture in 1959 her
designs recalled the mood of China, India and Japan with
themes that ranged from oriental filigree, fans, callig-
raphy, woodcarving, peacock feathers, bamboo and
blossoms. There was also the influence of the buildings

she had seen (Italian, Spanish, French, Greek) and the interiors she had frequented (Roman classic, Baroque, Rococo, Islamic and Renaissance). Her time on stage and the personality she had assumed also provided the impetus for a personal style that followed a 'more is more' mantra: more makeup, more colour, more jewellery, more layers, more fur. After her return from Shanghai, Florence always acted (and looked) as if she were on stage. She transformed herself to encapsulate the spirit of every era she lived through. The vamp of the twenties became the femme fatale in sleek dinner suits and silver fox fur wraps in the thirties; the forties saw her in military-style clothing— dramatic capes and pillbox hats; in the fifties her wardrobe was filled with corsets, trumpet skirts and pearls; in the sixties (when she herself was sixty) she wore pop-art mini-skirts and beehives; and in the seventies, despite Sydney's humidity and heat, she donned full-length mink coats and knee-high leather boots. Florence was invariably the dressiest woman in any room.

In 1927, Florence's alluring, theatrical and slightly scary appearance would have been nothing short of a shock to Mount Perry locals, whose idea of getting dressed up was to comb through some Brylcreem or pull on a pair of stockings. The memory the people of Mount Perry had of Florence and the Florence who returned from Shanghai were two different people. She could not have looked less like the girlish aspirant who had won eisteddfods and performed in Toowoomba's Smart Set Diggers. But as Florence saw things, it was in her heart and mind that the biggest changes had taken place.

Her self-esteem and self-assuredness were strong and they were assets that would remain constant throughout her life. Gone was the innocent wide-eyed youth who yearned for escape and adventure and in her place was a tough, wise and resilient woman who had had a bitter-sweet taste of the world. Not only was the trauma of war permanently etched on her mind, but she had achieved considerable success under sometimes dangerous and trying conditions—as a performer and as a business-woman. Never again could she be satisfied by life in a sleepy, rural town.

From her adventures, including her possible affair with Wallingford Tate, Florence now understood what she wanted from herself, from life and from others around her. She had caught a glimpse of her potential, of what was possible and what she could turn herself into.

Florence's family and friends had not ventured far beyond the realms of Mount Perry during her absence, but there had been a few changes. Her sister May was now a teacher at the Drummer's Creek School and, with her boyfriend, Bill, she had taken over residency at The Pines, the grandiose home and property purchased by the Broadhursts in 1930. Fassifern had settled down with a local girl and they had four children. Priscilla would have to wait another two years before she would walk down the aisle. Her marriage to Robert Hudson failed after only twelve months but spawned Priscilla's only child, Barbara.

Life for Florence's mother and father had also changed. They had, for the time being, abandoned cattle husbandry for hospitality. In 1923, Bill Broadhurst had signed the licence for the bustling Grand Hotel located in the heart of Mount Perry. Living there was an exciting, fast-paced lifestyle that suited Bill and they remained the licensees of the hotel for fifteen years.

The hotel, an imposing, colonial building that boasted two levels and wide wooden verandas that fronted a busy, dusty street, was also their new home. Built to accommodate thirty guests (today the new Grand Hotel in Mount Perry has only three rooms) the original hotel cast shadows over nearby businesses and the local council buildings. In the evening miners and farmers gathered there to drink and play billiards. Behind the bar, hotel maids in neck-to-ankle dresses, knee-high boots and hair rolled high in a bun, served the customers.

Florence helped her sister Priscilla behind the bar at the hotel. According to family friend Ted Bettiens it wasn't just the customers who were doing the drinking: 'When

Florence and Priscilla worked behind the bar they drank as much as they served.'

During 1927 Florence's many old friends and acquaintances dropped in for a cup of tea and a chat at the hotel. Some of them had qualified as nurses and teachers or worked at the local council. Others had married or moved away to Bundaberg or Brisbane. Very few of them had even left Queensland, let alone travelled abroad. Listening to Florence's tales of her intrepid adventures perhaps left them wondering at their own lives.

Soon Florence grew bored with the local chitchat, society musical evenings, dinner parties and playing tennis with May and Priscilla. She had made up her mind that she was going to London in October, but she hadn't yet decided what she was going to do when she got there. She vacillated between studying music and singing or undertaking a course in interior design. Her brief stay at home was precisely the medicine she needed. She had time to gather her strength without the pressure of a business to run or an atmosphere fraught with tension.

•

Florence had probably had something to drink on 31 July 1927, the day she took her father's brand new Studebaker car out for a spin. Two friends came along for the joy ride when Florence took the wheel. She had only just turned up Main Street when horrified onlookers saw the car sway about the road. In her panic, Florence put her foot on the accelerator instead of the brake and the car became airborne and turned two complete somersaults, throwing Florence violently out of the car. Her two companions escaped with 'a severe shaking'.

Florence's condition was considered serious. Not only did she sustain a fracture at the base of her skull, but she was covered in cuts and bruises. The wheels of the upturned car were still spinning when they whisked Florence away to the hospital. The car, whose radiator, windshield and hood were 'smashed in' was 'righted and put under the Federal Hall' (*Bundaberg Daily News and Mail*, 1927). The press covered the incident extensively. The headlines read, 'Mt Perry Sensation. Miss F. Broadhurst injured. Medical Aid from Bundaberg'; 'Queensland Actress Seriously Injured'; and 'Miss Broadhurst, In a Serious Motor Crash. Suffers Fractured Skull'. In a photo published in the *Bundaberg Daily News and Mail* on 31 July 1927, Florence's pale cat-like eyes peer out from underneath an elegant floral scarf pinning her hair down. The caption reads ' . . . not long home from world wandering, [Florence] met with disaster at the week-end through the overturning of the newly purchased car'.

LONDON

1927–1949

'Whatever the hour of the occasion, you could never be
safer than in a Pellier creation.'

ADVERTISEMENT FOR MADAM PELLIER'S MAYFAIR DRESS SALON

*F*lorence spent two-and-a-half long months recovering from the car accident and was lucky she didn't die. But that didn't change her plans to travel to London. Florence booked her ticket under her stage name, Bobby Broadhurst, and departed from the New Farm Wharf in Brisbane on 17 October 1927. It would be three weeks before the pint-sized ship, *The Orvieto*, finally left Australia's shores because it had more adventurers to collect from Sydney (where passengers from New Zealand joined the ship), Melbourne, Adelaide and Fremantle. It was from this Western Australian port on 7 November that the ship's captain finally navigated *The Orvieto* offshore on a 13 000-mile (about a 12 000-kilometre), six-week voyage that included such exotic ports as Ceylon, Port Said, Naples, Toulon, Gibraltar and Plymouth.

Florence's first-class cabin was in a handy spot, close to the main public rooms on the upper deck. Although it was sixty pounds more expensive than the third-class fee it was still basic: furnished with a bed, washstand, seat, wardrobe and not much else. But Florence didn't waste time rattling around in her constrained quarters. She preferred to occupy the lounge, the music room, the first-class smoking saloon or stroll along the promenade deck where there were frequent games of cricket, lawn tennis, quoits, bowls and hop-scotch to enjoy. The lounge—where passengers met to play the piano, read or eat—was typically Georgian, decorated in muted tones of grey and white, while French prints and Indian rugs provided theatrical sparks of colour. Here and there clusters of Italian walnut chairs and tables and richly upholstered sofas lit with opal globes provided a cosy retreat from the harsh winds that blew off the ocean. It was a space where passengers met—to an exacting routine—for meals four times daily. Colourful diversions to this schedule were provided with shore excursions to markets, museums, galleries, local restaurants, Sunday church choirs and theatrical evenings.

By the time Florence arrived in Britain in December 1928, the grey, bleak streets were banked with snow. When it wasn't snowing it was raining, and when it wasn't raining, low-hanging clouds were threatening to burst.

For Florence, gone were the *moderne* Shangainese women with their exaggerated makeup. Londoners had to brave the elements by dressing stylishly in high collars, long capes, coats and gloves. It was a look (incomplete without trompe-l'oeil epaulettes, flares, layers, buttons, zips, pillbox hats and false eyelashes) that was elitist and sophisticated, influenced by screen divas such as Greta Garbo, Marlene Dietrich and Ginger Rogers.

The twenties was a decade of visual change in Britain: there was a shift in style right across the arts, from fashion, to painting and architecture. Modernism, with its conflicting aesthetics, had arrived. Craftsmanship remained a strong ideal, but so was the trend to experiment (particularly in the realm of mass production) with new techniques and materials.

Conflicting visual aesthetics was not the only change taking place in Britain between the wars; this period also conjured up conflicting emotions. While women had discovered a new freedom in office jobs, factories and the like, many returning soldiers—despite the rhetoric of victory—were unemployed, bitter and uncertain about what lay ahead. And although many aspects of British life had started to crumble, the rigid class structure, with the educated middle and upper classes believing in their own moral and cultural superiority over the working classes, was still intact. Life in Britain was an improved version of the social divide between the haves and have-nots that Florence got used to while living in Shanghai.

Florence found a place to live at 22 Upper Gloucester Place, Dorset Square. At twenty-eight years of age, it was considered odd that she was unmarried and scandalous that she should travel across the globe by herself. But Florence cared little about social constraints and convention and her arrival in London marked a period of profound soul-searching. She developed an unquenchable thirst for philosophy, religion and ideology. Alex Graf, a friend from Kent, sent this letter to Florence which provides a glimpse of her new passion.

Dear Florence, What new philosophy have you adopted? You always had unusual ideas and an unusual way of expressing them—this is our affinity. I am terribly fed up with our hypocritical society and forever platitude blabbering politicians and churchmen. Everyone is brainwashed and conditioned, everyone is a conformist, individualism is tabu, and he who looks to the left while everyone is looking to the right is out of step, a misfit, a traitor. I realize that all I experience is my own projection—and in order to change the world I have to change myself. I do believe that all we are is the result of what we have thought and all that we shall be is the result of what we are thinking now. At least that gives us the chance to change the future to our liking. It is never too late and nothing is impossible, always Alex.

P.S. I found a lot of enlightenment in books by Krishnamurti and books about Zen.

Florence threw herself into her new interests with abandon. She filled scrapbooks, notebooks and diaries with newspaper clippings and quotes by evangelists, reverends, philosophers, scientists and novelists on themes that ranged from health and nature to faith. She was particularly enamoured with the writings of poet Patience Strong, whose favourite aphorism was 'Nothing's true unless you've lived it' and whose obituary claimed 'many a British serviceman perished with a cutting of a Patience Strong poem in the pocket of his battledress' (*Daily Telegraph*, 1990).

Lady Mary Ravensdale, who was not only the president of the World Congress of Faiths, but one of the first four women to become a member of the House of Lords in 1958, also inspired Florence. Lady Ravensdale (like Florence) was a bundle of contradictions. She was an outspoken and controversial member of Britain's aristocracy who displayed contempt for democracy, associating it with all things bourgeois, dull and inert (Sutherland, 1999). She did much to rally against a Labour government who claimed it would be wrong for women to engage themselves in politics 'by virtue of birth'. When Lady Ravensdale famously remarked that the male members of the House of Lords were 'a drowsy lot of flies buzzing comfortably in a warm room, afraid of the entry of a few hornets' it was an attack on those of her peers, such as Fred Pethick-Lawrence, who claimed that the raison d'être behind opposition to equal rights was that men dealt with women on an emotional plane, and it was impossible to think of them as colleagues. Likewise, Lord Glasgow stated lazily, 'We simply don't want [women] here. We don't want to meet them in the library or sit next to them on these benches. This is a house of men . . . we don't want a House of Lords and Ladies! This is the last place in the country where men can meet without women. For heaven's sake let us keep it that way!' (Sutherland, 1999).

Just as Sir Winston Churchill would later inspire Florence in the realm of politics and public speaking, Lady Ravensdale fuelled Florence's feminist leanings and inspired her increasingly unorthodox views on life.

Alongside Florence's carefully collected articles stuck into her scrapbooks, she jotted down personal musings on themes that included eternal youth, the power of the mind, positive self-talk and spiritual ideology. They ranged from single moments of clarity ('entertain only the nobler and more constructive emotions'; 'use the power of the

The cluster of huts at Mungy Station, Mount Perry Queensland, where Florence Maud Broadhurst was born on either 28 July or 26 August 1899. Mungy Station sprawled over an impressive 300 000 acres (approx. 122 000 hectares) in its heyday and is still a working cattle station today. It is probable that one of the horsemen in this shot was Florence's father, Bill Broadhurst, who managed the property for William Sly. A hut still stands in the exact location where Florence was born.

COURTESY PAT SMITH.

Florence was only eleven years old in 1910 when she joined the local Children's Tennis Club in Mount Perry with her sisters May and Priscilla. The three sisters inherited a passion for tennis (and competition) from their father, who was still serving and volleying in his eighties. Mount Perry tennis enthusiasts in this image include (left to right, top to bottom): Burnett Dingle, May Broadhurst, Ruby Renfrey, Ida Dingle, Nellie Paul, Percy Dingle, Florence Broadhurst, Henry Dingle, Priscilla Broadhurst, Ethel Hunter (holding baby Marion) and Tom Prior.

COURTESY PAT SMITH.

Florence with her sister Priscilla (Cilla) in Mount Perry, Queensland. This photograph was taken around 1918–20.

COURTESY PAT SMITH.

Florence and her friend Edna Raymond share a life buoy. It is probable this photo was taken when Florence was touring the East with the musical comedy troupe, The Globetrotters, in the mid-twenties.

COLLECTION: POWERHOUSE MUSEUM, SYDNEY, AUSTRALIA.

Florence in Poona, India, in the mid-twenties. When she was a member of The Globetrotters. The group travelled to and performed in many countries in Asia—India, Burma, Siam, Malaya and Japan among them.

Florence Broadhurst and Wallingford Tate share a tourer in Malaysia. Wallingford was a fellow Globetrotter member and special friend of Florence's.

Florence (seated, bottom left) on a weekend away with friends in Malaysia, in the mid-twenties. Harry Reynolds kneels beside her. Standing from left to right are Alfred Dicks, Edna Raymond and Wallingford Tate.

Florence (bottom right) on ship deck, in the mid-twenties, with members of the comedy musical troupe, The Globetrotters, and other friends. Wallingford Tate stands behind Florence at top right. Harry Reynolds and Edna Raymond sit beside Florence.

On 15 February 1926, Florence launched the 'Broadhurst Academy Incorporated School of the Arts' in Shanghai. To attract students to the academy, which provided tuition in all forms of dance, music and elocutionary studies, Florence hosted frequent dance demonstrations. She is seen here with her assistant, Mr Gleron, demonstrating the dance steps of the Charleston.

MITCHELL LIBRARY, SLNSW.

THE CULT OF THE CHARLESTON.—Miss Bobbie Broadhurst and her partner, tutors from the Broadhurst Academy who demonstrated the Charleston and the Tango at the French Club Sunday evening. Miss Broadhurst is Principal of the Broadhurst Academy, 38 Kiangse Road.

A 27-year-old Florence, as she appeared in the Shanghai Sunday Times *on 27 February 1927, after organising a concert at the British Women's Association headquarters in Shanghai. This concert was one of many performances Florence organised around the city in the twenties, including a number of soirees for Major General John Duncan and his British troupes.*

MITCHELL LIBRARY, SLNSW.

ORGANIZES SUCCESSFUL CONCERT.—Miss B. Broadhurst, A.T.C.L., who was responsible for the highly successful concert given at the B.W.A. headquarters Friday week. Assisting artists were Messrs. Kitain Bros., Ralph Lynn, Higgerman and Walford, and the Misses Peggy James and Bell Leichner.—*Photo by Porter Studio.*

This image of Dick Norton's Globetrotters appeared alongside a performance review in the Manchuria Daily News *on 28 March 1924. The troupe vacillated between six and nine members—depending on which review you read—and included Dick Crichton, Florence 'Bobby' Broadhurst, Charles Holt, Wallingford Tate, Kitty Farrell, Leila Forbes, Dorothy Drew, Ralph Sawyer and Dick Norton. Florence is seated on the piano.*

Right: Florence masquerading as her alter ego 'Bobby' Broadhurst. This image appeared in the Shanghai Sunday Times *in the mid-twenties. The caption read: 'Miss Broadhurst added zest to Carlton's Xmas Programme. She is the possessor of a rich soprano voice, and holds all the characteristics of a smart musical comedy artist.'*

Opposite: An advertisement for The Broadcasters, a musical comedy group that Florence joined in 1924. Other members included Wallingford Tate, Jack Crighton and Beryl Lucina. The Broadcasters toured the East and performed at Shanghai-based venues including the Star Theatre, the French Club and the Carlton Club. Florence appears as 'Bobby' Broadhurst in the bottom right hand corner.

MISS BOBBY BROADHURST

Florence the stage siren appears centre stage in this dramatic image from the Lloyd's Weekly, Shanghai. *This photograph, of the Carlton Sparklers, was taken during Florence's final week with the troupe after a successful season as the singing lead.*

Florence masquerading as Madame Pellier—the identity she adopted while living in London. The origins of the name remain a mystery, as in 1933—when this article appeared in London's Town and Country News—*Florence was married to her first husband, Percy Kann. The article, 'For the Woman of Refinement', features details of Florence's Mayfair dress salon, Pellier Ltd.*

mind, courage and self control' and 'form habits known to contribute to the welfare of the mind and the body') to long rambling entries on topics such as 'The universal intelligence we call God, or more intimately and lovingly "our father who art in heaven" is the supreme source of perfect health and youth' and 'As Ralph Waldo Emerson says, while we commune with that which is above us, we grow young.' Her preoccupation with looking and feeling younger was a theme that continued throughout Florence's life. And it seemed as if she had doctors on a pedestal. As she wrote in her diary, 'A surgeon—His characteristics in his profession were accuracy, dexterity and gentleness of touch. He was a man of acute sympathies who was greatly distressed by human suffering. His understanding was appreciated by his students that they went to him for a solution to their private and personal difficulties.' She even recorded jokes about them: 'The man who consulted his doctor to see who could advise him what to do in order that he should live to 100. So the doctor replies give up drinking, smoking and women and he said then shall I live to 100 and the doctor replied no but it will feel like it.' In more personal moments in her scrapbooks, Florence reflects on her childhood in Mount Perry and notes: 'I would recommend more enlightenment of spiritual life should be given at an early age—in plain understandable language—not hinted at or presented as being expounded from a Bible quotation but clearly defined—the advantages of living a god-like existence . . .'

But Florence was no angel. On the contrary, many of the quotes that she either collected or invented were tainted with sexual overtones, including 'what a girl needs is a bad influence'; 'I see a throbbing vitality'; 'power and lust of the mind' and the unusual, almost disturbing, entry 'what is the difference between rape and seduction?'

Of all the hand-written entries, the most startling and the one that provides us with a piercing insight into her lifelong habit of reinventing herself and acting out roles, is titled 'Personality Building'. It is unclear whether Florence undertook a transcendental course of sorts or whether she invented the theory that follows. These (pages upon pages) of hastily scribbled notes instruct the reader that human beings are an 'ever renewing and ever unfolding expression of the infinite life'. She provides five steps or 'spiritual rules' on 'building a personality'. These include 'Rule 1—Learn to Build a New Personality'. This rule incorporates four stages, namely: Suggestions, Impersonation, Personification and Embodiment and Assumption. In 'learning to build a new personality' students are introduced to 'suggest characteristics of personality— concentrate and visualise with faith and confidence that you may become the happy, winning magnetic personality you would love to be' while the 'impersonation' step

instructs students to 'begin to act out the part [they] have strongly suggested to the subconscious mind'.
The other rules follow:

> Rule 2: Educate yourself thoroughy [sic] for success.
> Rule 3: Seek to express in your outer life the nobility, power and beauty of your inner life.
> Rule 4: Study and observe so that you will know how to read and understand people.

This process of 'personality building' came naturally to Florence. Her discovery (or invention) of the 'rules' merely served to reinforce what she was already thinking and *doing*. She had instinctively morphed into Bobby, the singing dancing coquette, by pretending she was British. Then later, during her time in London, she transformed herself into Madame Pellier, the Mayfair couturier. When she returned to Australia from London, she reinvented herself again as the Australian doyenne of design. Florence's manifesto on 'Personality Building' paints a picture of a single-minded woman with an inquiring mind who was determined to be successful, even if it meant *turning into someone else*.

Florence's musings, press clippings and notes were certainly not isolated to the realm of subconscious persuasion. Many were rehashed and presented in her numerous talks on the place of women in world affairs that Florence delivered as a voluntary speaker for the Women-for-Westminster Movement and a member of the Conservative Party's panel of speakers. An author who was a source of inspiration for Florence's public speaking from this period was Ethel Mannin, a self-confessed 'emancipated, rebellious, and angry young woman' (Princess Grace Irish Library, 2001).

Ethel's books examined the lives of working-class women and anarchism and pacifism in the forties. She reputedly had an affair with the poet W.B. Yeats. An article by Mannin, published in the *Daily Express* on 18 September 1928, was part of a series that invited writers, playwrights, psychologists and scientists to discuss 'their faith' in the 'things they believe in most implicitly'. On the rambling (and now somewhat faded) yellow press clipping, Florence highlighted phrases that appealed to her, including: 'Power and glory pass with the years, but the spirit of beauty remains. Beauty is the thread of intelligence running through the chaos and confusion of the vast tapestry of life'; 'The emotional reaction to beauty as expressed in music, painting, sculpture and poetry, derives from precisely the same source as profound emotional reactions to personalities', and 'I do not believe that art is a luxury of civilisation; I believe it is a vital necessity for the making of civilisation endurable.'

A speech that Florence delivered while living in Sydney in the fifties draws on Mannin's theme. Her version reads: 'Art and creation is synonymous with beauty. It is the emotional reaction to beauty that compels those who have the ability to create to pour out that emotion in song, in words or poetry, literature or architecture.' And drawing on Ethel's 'vast tapestry of life' theme, Florence writes: 'I weave my defence from this loom.'

The late twenties also marked a period when Florence fancied herself as a fiction writer. One of the poetic entries in her notebook included:

After they had eaten, the two men light their pipes and then commenced to talk. He explained that he studied the language and the habits of the Indians and that he was going to write on the subject a large book of 20 volumes. That was the object of his voyage to Alaska. He did not add that the first chapter was not yet started.

Another read:

A serene sky, and sea that, as it swirls round the rocks deepens to the colour of crushed butterflies wings and above the strength and splendour of the guardian cliffs . . . there was a kind of healing benediction.

She also philosophised about life and pondered the fabric of society. At times she painted a bitter, cynical picture of the world around her, while at other times she was overwhelmed by its beauty and joy. Trying to make sense out of the bipolar views she presented is a daunting task. One entry read:

> Progress of civilisation is made possible only by vigorous sometimes even violent lying; that the social contract is nothing more or less than a vast conspiracy of human beings . . . Lies are the mortar that bind the individual man into the social masonry. What is man? Lust and greed tempered by fear and irrational vanity.

And another:

> It has always been my conviction that the world belongs not to princes, not to the politicians, not even to the merchants, whose caravans wind their way to so many Baghdad's but to the gentle band of [this word is indecipherable], who can gaze into the heart of a flower and behold the secret of the universe.

For those who might feel they were close to unlocking the key to Florence's mind, she offered up this food for thought:

> Beyond the ken of the printed word are vast sources of thought and spiritual refreshment which in these

days of universal education fewer and fewer of us feel the impulse to explore.

•

Shortly after Florence arrived in London she met Percy Walter Gladstone Kann. To Florence, Percy was everything that Wallingford was not. He was worldly, sophisticated and wealthy. He had a career ahead of him and led the high life. Various reports claim that Percy was either a prince (there were rumours that he was connected to the Spencer family), a stockbroker, Pakistani, or connected to the English gentry. When she went out with Percy, Florence did not perform to monarchs and the upper echelons, she mixed with them at dinner and cocktail parties and sat in the royal box at such venues as the Wembley Stadium and Greyhound Racecourse. Among her personal papers there is a photograph of Florence having afternoon tea with the Queen Mother. This friendship would endure, at least on a social level, until the fifties. Whenever Florence and the monarch found themselves at the same social event (which did not occur infrequently), they always took time out to have a quick chat.

In 1929, after only a year and a half in London, Florence and Percy married on 22 June. The wedding was a lavish affair, with no expenses spared. In a photo taken in the Kensington Gardens, Florence is wearing an elaborate wedding frock, an elegant headpiece and carrying an impractically large bouquet of roses and cascading greenery that threatens to overshadow her gown. A filmy white veil falls about her shoulders and the length of her back. In its transparent beauty, Florence looks almost angelic.

The wedding was held at one of the most impressive churches in London, the Church of the Immaculate Heart of St Mary (commonly known as the Brompton Oratory), located on Brompton Road in South Kensington. It is an extraordinary church for a number of reasons: it is the second-largest Roman Catholic church in London, it has a regal Italianate style that is rarely seen in Britain, and though it was constructed in the 1880s, the interior contains elements that hark back to the 1660s. It was against this lustrous backdrop of marble, precious stones, mosaic tiles and stone carvings that Florence, Percy and their witness, known only as A. Lewis Leighton, signed the wedding certificate. It stated Florence was twenty-seven years old. In fact she was twenty-nine. (Stretching the truth about her age was something that Florence continued to do until she was well into her seventies. As a friend recalled at the time of her death, 'When Florence was seventy-eight, she said she was forty-eight.')

The newlyweds travelled to Paris where they frittered money away at gambling houses such as the Casino de la Foret and played sport at Le Touquet de Tennis. Whether

Florence and Percy actually lived in Paris for a time or not is unclear. Florence herself lost track of the web of inconsistencies that she concocted about her life with Percy. In one article, 'She came to Rest and Stayed to Paint', written about her when she returned to Australia in the fifties, Florence claims she spent 'ten years studying in Paris' and the 'next ten years in England'. In another article Florence contradicts this and says, 'I didn't go to Paris to paint at all, I was training as a singer'. And later she remembered that she did go to Paris after all, to paint. 'I spent time in Paris painting landscapes on the left bank,' she said. However, it is unlikely Florence spent 'ten years studying in Paris' for a number of reasons: she arrived in London in 1927; married Percy at the Brompton Oratory in 1929; launched a Mayfair couturier business with Percy in the early thirties; and met her second husband, Leonard Lloyd Lewis, in 1935.

Florence sometimes fancied herself as a scholar. According to Florence she was a one-time associate of the London Trinity College of Music, as well as a student at London's Slade School of Fine Art, but there are no records to confirm this story which was published in the *Daily Telegraph* in 1977. Florence certainly studied painting (her many exhibitions in Sydney throughout the fifties and sixties, and her considerable drafting skills, provide testimony to this), but the exact location of her studies might never be known. Florence kept sketch books from this era that she filled with dimensional doodles and handwritten notes pressed firmly into the page that read, for example: 'On Painting a Picture—first determine where the light is coming from to fix the shadow, to work out full character of shadow'; and 'Notes of Importance— Strokes—Press and Relax with several colours. Use different colour to underline corners for more forms.'

Florence (who left her 'rank of profession' void on her wedding certificate) also claimed that she was a London-based interior designer. In an article published in the *Australian Women's Weekly* in 1965, she described what she sold in her 'interior decorating' store in London. 'When we couldn't get anything, I bleached Hessian bags and decorated them with raffia and shells—they made wonderful lampshades. We used sailcloth and dyed arti-ficial sheets too,' she said. Florence did make one remark, however, that goes some way to helping us sort out this tangle of deception. She said, 'It was partly my interest in clothes which showed me how easily I could express myself in line and colour. I studied and painted, and earned some money designing clothes.'

•

In the early thirties, Florence and Percy launched a cou-turier on the corner of New Bond and Brook streets in

Mayfair, London. Advertisements for the shop—originally known as Kann and Pellier—claim it was a 'dress house' that supplied 'better clothes at lower prices', with Florence acting as a 'designer and dress consultant to film and stage'. According to an article that appeared in *Town and Country News* on 8 December 1933 'its numerous regulars' included 'many notable figures of the stage and society'. Some of these regulars might have included stage and screen divas such as Valerie Hobson, Googie Withers, Dame Gracie Fields, Dame Wendy Hiller or Phyllis Calvert. Others might have included the wives and lovers of Stewart Granger, Val Guest, Harold French, Sir Michael Balcon, Marius Goring and the like. And given the social connections that Florence and Percy had forged for themselves, it appears at least one member of the royal family came to have her frocks fitted at Florence's shop.

The shop itself—'one of the outstanding successes of London's dress world'—was elegant but spartan, with art-deco appeal. A number of carpeted salons and private change rooms were hidden behind heavy velvet drapes and the rest of the elegant space was scattered with dresses on metal stands, pendant lamps, vases of flowers, hand mirrors and comfortable upholstered sofas. As the article points out, the shop was 'presided over by a lady who herself is a genuine dress artist, and who is one of the most original of dress designers'.

Accompanying the article is a photo of Florence—at this point in time a raven-haired beauty—wearing a simple dress with a keyhole neckline with her signature kohl-lined eyes, dark lips and swept back shingle hairstyle. Underneath the photo is her name. Not Florence or Bobby Broadhurst. Not Florence Kann. But her newest nom de guerre: Madame Pellier. Florence was again attempting to conceal her Queensland past. Was her transformation as Madame Pellier an exercise in 'personality building' or a media stunt designed to draw clientele into a shop presided over by a sophisticated European dress designer, not an Australian sheila from a cattle station? Either way, the successful enterprise soon became synonymous with the force of Florence's new 'personality' and, although Percy remained one of the salon's co-directors, it wasn't long before 'Kann and Pellier' lost the name Kann and 'Pellier Ltd' was born.

Florence, whose second husband called her 'the first of the women's libbers', claims she did a roaring trade among the upper crust. One of her designs—a long wool coat with accentuated epaulettes—featured in *Vogue* magazine on 27 November 1935. The elegant illustration features a woman wearing a pillbox hat, a coat with a high collar around the face and carrying a clutch purse, bearing the caption, 'Colourful plaid outlines. This navy wool coat, 8 guineas, Pellier, Bond Street'. A brochure circulating at this time also features Florence (or rather Madame Pellier) looking decidedly French, wearing a beret tilted to one side and a dark jacket with a high neckline. A brochure for the shop from Florence's personal papers reads:

Paris via Pellier. Paris being Paris, is sometimes a little over-confident . . . flinging into the picture new modes that neither the English mind can cherish nor the English figure wear. A Frenchwoman can sometimes go to extremes in style and pattern that would make her English cousin look 'fancy dress'. This season, France, as you know, is going everything from Abyssinian to Bersaglieri . . . with military millinery . . . Renaissance gownery . . . classical negligee. And 'shirring' and 'draping' are becoming the most over-worked words in the couturier's vocabulary. All very whimsical and smart . . . MODERATION. Which is precisely where Madame Pellier sweeps in. The new Pellier models are founded on Paris but interpreted into smartest possible English. All that the Pellier models have lost is a danger of looking ridiculous. And ah, how much they have gained! Whatever the hour of the occasion, you could never be safer than in a Pellier creation.

•

While she was still married to Percy a twenty-three-year-old named Leonard Lloyd Lewis came into Florence's dress salon in 1935. What the young Londoner was doing hanging around a fancy women's dress salon is anybody's guess, but he described his 'storybook meeting' with Florence in an *Australian Women's Weekly*'s interview in 1977:

> We met completely by chance . . . I was a good-looking twenty-three and Florence was a glamorous thirty-six. It was like a young man meeting a film star. I was instantly enamoured. I didn't leave her side for twenty-six years,' he says. As Leonard explained, 'Florence's marriage to her first husband . . . was on shaky ground. Soon after we met she and Percy were divorced and we were married in London before the war.

Leonard was a financier, a diesel engineer or both. And, as his son Robert claimed, he was wealthy. Margaret Alcock, contributor to *Vogue Entertaining and Travel*, who befriended Leonard in the sixties, described him as, 'Effusive, lively, good humoured and kind. He always had good things to say about people. He was high spirited and socially gregarious.' Other people such as Leslie Walford described him less flatteringly as 'walking in Florence's shadow'. Leonard himself said, 'Wherever she went she was always Florence Broadhurst and I was acknowledged as "Mr Broadhurst". She didn't belong to any man.'

Leonard's marriage to Florence was fiery, extravagant and fuelled with passion. According to Margaret Alcock, Leonard was an extremely generous man. As Leonard explained, 'In the wonderful years of our marriage it gave me great pleasure to shower her with expensive jewellery. Florence, a dazzling woman herself, loved her equally dazzling jewels.' They were gifts more often than not accompanied by notes. Some were simple—'All my love Leonard'—while others were more effusive:

My lovely, it was lovely to see you last night. It makes me feel better when you come. You looked the best woman in the world to me last night. I believe you had love in your eyes. You mean so much to me. I don't think I could go on without you. Without you there would be nothing in life left. While I am writing to you now I feel as though you were sitting next to me, speaking to me. It's an odd feeling really. I feel I could tell you all I want to without writing. I love you with undying affection and my devotion to you will get stronger day by day. God bless you dearest. With all my love—Yours forever, Leonard.

•

Back in Mount Perry in Queensland, Florence's mother had been struggling with a heart condition for some time, and spent a month in hospital before passing away. The closest Florence got to the funeral was a letter she received from her sister May, written on 18 October 1938:

Dear Florence, Mother passed away last night after a month in hospital. Saturday evening she became unconscious and remained so for forty-eight hours with Dad and I by her bedside the whole time, but she never spoke just gasped away. It was a dreadful trying time. We had an impressive service in the crowded church and the funeral moved from there at three o'clock with the coffin smothered in lovely wreaths. I did all I could and the hospital staff was marvellous also Doctor yet that swelling I told you of was beyond human cures. It was the last stage of heart trouble the outcome of bad circulation and so she just had to lie each day only to get weaker. It was a terrible end I think. Dad is greatly grieved and broken up. Love May.

Margaret was buried at the Mount Perry cemetery, a haunting spot on a hillside that catches the sun. Bill was buried next to his wife in 1957. And later, when May and Priscilla died, they were buried beside their parents.

•

Hitler invaded Poland in 1939 and just the year before, in 1938, Florence's only son, Robert, was born on 3 May. The aerial bombardment of London at the beginning of World War II was the backdrop to her mothering. Anti-aircraft rockets, search beacons and flames rose from neighbourhoods, docks and industrial districts. A German bomb levelled the *Vogue* office, which had so keenly promoted Pellier products. It was a war that left 30 000 Londoners dead, 50 000 injured, destroyed the historic heart of the city and heralded a downward spiral for the fashion industry that was Florence's bread and butter.

Gone were the days of decadent fashion—economic responsibility and social rules heralded a new austerity. Britain buckled down to the rationing of cloth, clothing and footwear, while the British government battled to keep the fashion industry alive. In 1942 leading British designers launched a utility wardrobe that was all about conserving and recycling fabric. Uniform and mono-chromatic, the wartime garb placed an emphasis on accessories. These were difficult times for even the most robust business. The result was the closure, in the late thirties, of Pellier Ltd, Florence's famous fashion house that had once catered to the razzle-dazzle of customers from the stage and society. Once again war had destroyed

Florence Broadhurst's dream. Once again she was forced to move on.

•

From the early forties until her return to Sydney in 1949, Florence engaged in a mish-mash of endeavours, some charitable, some profitable: repatriation work, voice recordings at the British Broadcasting Corporation, operating a passenger boat from Brighton, managing her second husband's diesel engineering business in Surrey (strangely named F.M. Lewis Diesel Engineers after Florence) and homemaking. Leonard and Florence were now living at 12 Higher Drive, Banstead, Surrey. They generously opened their home to Australian airmen during the war and their efforts did not go unnoticed. A letter from London's Australia House in 1945 reads:

> Dear Mrs Lewis, Now that the war has come to an end and the Australian forces have practically all returned to Australia, it has been decided to close the Boomerang Club as of 13th December next. In this farewell message, I should like to say to you how deeply we, the members of the Australian Women's Voluntary Service, have appreciated the hospitality which you have extended to Australians throughout the War.

In the late forties the Lloyd Lewis family moved home to 26 Mill Road, Worthing. It was a house in a state of disrepair. With a child and husband to look after and a home to resurrect, Florence had her hands full. Not long after they moved in, Florence arranged for overgrown roses to be uprooted, the chimney to be repaired and a porous room to be removed. She took down faded curtains, removed broken brackets, tossed out panes of glass, installed new furniture and replaced tiles, washers and lights. Just one of the quotes for interior design hardware was addressed to 'F.M. Lewis Diesel Engineers', and came to a total of one hundred and eight pounds and four guineas. The list included:

3-piece suite
Fit curtain rod, brackets, railways, pelmet boards and hand 9 curtains
21 net curtains, hand hemmed
Double devan cover to match
4 tapestry curtains and lining
Braid and fringe to match
55 yds rufflette tape

When Florence had a moment to spare, she painted dozens of colourful canvases to adorn the walls of her new Worthing home.

•

Being just a homemaker and mother would never satisfy someone like Florence Broadhurst. She looked for opportunities wherever she went and she soon turned her attention to operating a charter boat. A letter from the former operator outlines the terms of the contract:

> I Raymond Kenneth Cook Smith of 17 Ham Road, Shoreham-by-Sea, hereby agree to allow Mrs. FM Lewis of 26 Mill Road Worthing, Sussex, the right to operate a "Slow Passenger" Boat from the West Pier at Brighton for the duration of a contract now in existence between myself and the West Pier Co., Ltd Brighton.

While operating a charter boat wasn't quite the same as running the performing arts school in Shanghai or the dress salon in Mayfair, the mood in post-war Britain was not about luxury, but necessity.

Then, in May 1949, when Robert was ten years old, Florence and Leonard made the decision to return to Australia. Their reasoning was that it was a better place to raise a child. The day that the Lloyd Lewises were scheduled to depart, the neon lights in Piccadilly Square were switched back on for the first time since the war. As Robert had never seen them before, his parents took him to look at them just before they sailed.

$\mathscr{S}$YDNEY

1949—1958

*'It's a risk for a woman to go alone into the desert,
but I've been lucky.'*

FLORENCE BROADHURST, 1954

On a glary, hot day at Manly Beach, Sydney, it's hard to see where the sun ends and the sand begins. Diamonds of light dance across the ocean as surfers carve gracefully through thick-lipped waves. From their towers in the sand, bronzed lifesavers keep a keen eye on swimmers and children squeal in delight as they leap from wooden wharves into harbour pools.

In the shade of Manly's resplendent promenade of pines, the newly arrived Lloyd Lewises would have peered out onto this quintessential Australian beach scene. Women paraded along the esplanade in fringed bathing suits and men wolf-whistled from behind the wheels of their convertible Chevrolets. Although the sun's uplifting radiance begged for the exposure of more flesh, the mood on Australian beaches was still restrained. Abbreviated

'French type' swimming costumes, known as bikinis, were considered scandalous in 1949. In 1945 the Manly Council, along with other Sydney Councils, tried to ban bikinis from its beaches. And as late as 1954 a woman was ordered off the beach at Manly when she dared to wear one.

After the war, Australia was nirvana compared to Britain. Manly village was bustling with glittering department stores, hotels decorated in art deco style, cafés and an abundance of shops filled with fresh produce, meat and fancy clothes. By 1947 ambitious schemes were afoot to transform Manly into a glitzy international tourist mecca and rumours were circulating that Mayor Merv Paine was negotiating to build a Disneyland at North Head. The fifties was an era of reinvention and dramatic change in Manly: bulldozers were busy demolishing old mansions, run-down cottages and slums to make way for a new generation of apartment blocks, fancy multi-storey hotels and dramatic high-rises that architect W.E. Beck believed would 'add to Manly's prestige'. Engineer Les Graham agreed with Beck's vision. The Manly he imagined had an oceanfront 'lined with glittering hotels and shops behind Manly's famous pine tree plantations' (Curby, 2001).

Australia as a whole was also on the precipice of great change. A new newspaper called the *Sun-Herald* announced that the Chifley government had been defeated and a new Liberal–Country Party, with Robert Menzies at the helm, had been sworn in.

•

Florence did not look fifty and neither did she act it. She had boundless energy. Her demeanour was swift, brusque and urgent. As Florence herself said, 'Man is not intended for the placid existence of a cow at pasture or the static complacency of a turnip in its furrow.' To cut her ties with her life in Britain she wrote a letter to 'H.G. Scadgell—complete hotel and house furnishings' in Montague Street, Worthing, requesting that the auctioneers sell her furniture and send her the proceeds. She also arranged to have some of her jewellery insured at a local Manly jeweller. Some of her dazzling gems included diamond and ruby earrings, a diamond brooch, a pearl necklace, and a diamond and ruby watch. Collectively they were worth two thousand five hundred and eighty nine pounds. (Later, in 1956, she insured a two-carat emerald and diamond cluster ring at Hardy Brothers on Castlereagh Street. It was worth three hundred and seventy pounds and it is probable that this was the same ring that Florence had stolen from her on the day that she was murdered.) On her travels through Europe Florence had also amassed a collection of antique jewellery. Actress and author Kate Fitzpatrick, who, along with her sister Sally, dyed her hair bright henna red in the sixties to look like Florence, remembered:

> She had a gold necklace made of Louis XV coins that, according to Florence, was one of three of its kind in the world. I had never seen anything like it before and Florence always carried it with her in her handbag. I think it was stolen from her when she died. Years later I saw a guy walking along Oxford Street in Paddington with one of the coins on a chain around his neck, and I remember looking at it and thinking that is weird.

One reporter made this comment on Florence's jewellery in the sixties:

> Unusual Accessories: They belong to Mrs. L Lewis—who collects antique gold pieces—and are from, top to bottom, a solid gold chain made in Czarist Russia (she calls it "her meal ticket"), another chain hung with antique coins from 19th century France, Austria, Hungary, England, Russia and Sardinia.

More than insuring her precious jewellery collection, Florence's return to Australia heralded a time to turn her attention elsewhere. She had a new home, life and career to establish. Florence decided she was going to be an artist. Her new home was a modern apartment on Victoria Parade located on the isthmus between leafy Manly village and the headland. It had the expansive Tasman Sea to the east, and a sheltered North Harbour to the west. The sandy stretch of Manly Beach was a mere stroll away, and so was Cabbage Tree Bay with its curious rock pools, and Manly Cove with its wharves that jut out like fingers over the water was also nearby. In one of the rooms of her new home Florence set up a painting studio. An article Florence kept from this period explained her thinking: 'Miss Broadhurst, who studied painting in Britain and France, originally meant to devote her time to singing. Soon the desire to submit her visual impressions to canvas took possession of her.'

Florence's daily routine was executed with military precision. From seven o'clock in the morning Florence would spend six hours at the easel where she worked at lightning speed. According to one reviewer, 'hers is a bizarre brush wielded with the speed of a comet . . . she has her signature on a large canvas inside two hours'.

To add depth and luminosity to the hundreds of paintings that were soon spilling from her studio, Florence used a technique employed by the early Italian school: tempera paint applied to the base of the canvas and oil paint on the top. Florence's painting style also had an antipodean thumbprint. One article states: 'out among the gum trees and Australia's historical buildings she (had) turned impressionist because she realised that cubism and futurism were insufficient to express what she felt about Australia' (*Australia Magazine*, 1954). Art critic James Gleeson described her work in glowing terms: 'Vim, bustle, enthusiasm, confidence, color and industry are the components of Miss Broadhurst's style,' he said.

Though Lloyd Rees, William Dobell, Russell Drysdale, Roland Wakelin, James Gleeson and Sidney Nolan were doing a more than adequate job of painting Australian landscapes, Florence was confident enough with her talent to remark that Australia had 'never before been properly shown on canvas. My oil paintings give a new angle on Australia' (*Australia Magazine*, 1954). She claimed that her new 'mission in life' was to 'add to the knowledge that people have of Australia' and she hoped her 'pictures may encourage more British migrants to come here'.

Painting gave Florence an outlet for her creative appetite that she once described as her lifeline. As she put it, 'I was once asked "How do you know you are living?" and I said, "I create so I know I am living"' (*Australian Home Journal*, 1968). Florence's art career also provided her with financial independence from Leonard who was described in the Australian press at this time as a London financier. By 1954 her bold paintings were selling for up to eighty guineas each.

Florence was determined to avoid becoming like the average Australian female in the fifties who was either supported by her husband or earning seventy-five per cent of the average male wage. As Florence maintained,

> The outstanding feature of Australian life is the huge number of worthy causes subscribed to by women who have no allowance from their husbands or income of their own, yet manage to make sacrifices from their weekly budget to support the many calls that are made upon them. Women are the sculptors of the human race.

When Florence wasn't painting in her studio, she spent her days sketching scenes on the beaches around Manly and on the busy streets in the village or she made the trek up to the headland where she studied the rambling greenery and the plunging cliffs. Other days she took a short ferry ride into the heart of Sydney and explored the sights of the Botanical Gardens and the glittering stretch of Sydney Harbour. But as Florence was becoming more proficient as an artist, she sought different subjects to paint so, in 1950, Florence carted her easel and sunhat to rural towns such as Richmond, Bathurst, Forbes and Orange.

Florence had the freedom to go where she wanted, when she wanted and for as long as she wanted. After all, there was nothing (and no one) keeping her at home. In July 1950, just a few months after they arrived on the ship from London, Florence and Leonard had sent Robert to board at one of Sydney's most prestigious boys' schools, Barker College. He was in sixth grade by then and a good student, who excelled in sport. Even though sport was compulsory at the school, with well over half the students involved in sporting activities such as rugby and cricket, Robert relished his time on the playing field. In 1952 he was a member of the Under 14A XV rugby team, as well as the captain of the Under 14B XI cricket team. And in 1953 he kicked some goals playing for the 15A XV rugby team. Robert remained a boarder at Barker College until December 1954, when he was in fourth form.

Even before her son was born, Florence had imagined what sort of life she wanted to carve out for Robert. High on her list was a good education, self assurance, practicality and a sense of direction and of self worth. As Florence herself said, 'The ideal society is one which offers each individual the precious chance of self fulfilment— the chance to be happy, to serve, to achieve.' In her London diaries she surmised that if she ever had a son, she would:

. . . want him to meet girls of his own age throughout his school career, to rid him of that curse of self-consciousness in the presence of women that has been such a handicap to many decent men. I am so tired of people in this world who are forever standing on their dignity. What a lot they miss, how they behave in their small mean minds.

Later she mused:

Marriage is such a final responsibility. For my son, I should struggle to see that everything in his teaching and environment at school would induce him to believe in his terms, that the consummation of a man's destiny is rather marriage than material gains. At the same time, by all means, let his education be a practical one. Let him be taught how to type, to write in shorthand, to answer the telephone, to darn his own socks, to cook, how to dance and how to play tennis.

Although Florence had high expectations of the sort of adult she wanted Robert to turn into, it is probable that mother and son had their differences. As ex-employee, Sally Fitzgerald pointed out, 'I worked for Florence for four years and I only met Robert twice. Florence told me she would never leave her wallpaper business to Robert.' David

Miles, an architectural draughtsman who later set up David Miles Handprints in opposition to Florence's wallpaper business reckoned, 'I'm not sure what it was all about, but Florence didn't speak to Robert for years. She went through a stage where she completely wiped him out of her life.' It seems tension also existed between Robert and Leonard. Among Florence's personal papers at the State Library of New South Wales is a letter from an exasperated Leonard, who was in Canberra at the time, saying:

> I will not ring from Canberra, tell Robert not to ring me, I shall not speak to him . . . I hate to tell you what has happened sweetheart but this cannot go on.

With Robert at school and Leonard busy with work, Florence filled her car with fuel, packed a tent, sleeping bags, maps, clothes, wash tubs and painting paraphernalia and hit the road in search of scenes that inspired her. Though Leonard and Robert initially accompanied her on these trips (as Florence put it, 'I'll paint and they'll fish'), they journeyed with her less and less frequently. Florence occasionally asked a girlfriend to come along, but she soon realised that she achieved more (and had the sort of trip she wanted) if she went alone.

Her trips started as long weekends, then grew into weeks, fortnights and sometimes months in duration. In

1954 one of her journeys took three months from start to finish. From the early fifties onward, there weren't many places in Australia she didn't go, but she concentrated on the Northern Territory, Central Australia and Queensland. She always returned with dozens of canvases and sketchbooks filled with images of lush green canefields, fields of dried grass, street scenes, orange groves, tropical fruits and old stone houses with crumbling brick chimney stacks, which charmed her because 'they're so unlike anything English' (*Australia Magazine*, 1954).

On a trip to Queensland with Leonard in 1954, Florence revisited her childhood haunts: Maryborough, Bundaberg, Childers, the Bunya Mountains and the Great Barrier Reef. She even returned home to Mount Perry where she and Leonard pitched a tent by the creek near The Pines. While there, Florence set up her easel in the main street of Mount Perry and painted a large canvas of the Grand Hotel with electricity poles marching along a red and treeless street. The undulating countryside of her father's Elliot's Creek property is a feature toward the rear of the painting.

On her return to Sydney, Florence's only remark about her painting of the Grand Hotel, reproduced in full colour in the *Australia Magazine* in 1954, was a dismissive one: 'There's always an old hotel you know,' she said simply. The article, titled 'Ambassadress with a Paintbrush', introduced Florence as 'an Englishwoman, who came to Australia five years ago to escape Britain's grey sky and rationing'. A comment from Florence follows: 'Every day is a painter's day in this country. In Britain you can paint on a few days only because the weather is usually too bad to set up your canvas outside.' Interestingly, Florence made no reference to her Mount Perry childhood, the existence of her family, or Bill, who at this point was very ill (he died three years later). According to Ted Bettiens, it was 'a thorn in Bill's side' that Florence so blatantly 'dismissed her Queensland past'.

By 1954, Florence estimated that she had travelled more than 20 000 miles (about 32 000 kilometres) throughout the Australian outback. A large part of this distance was clocked up when she went on a three-month-long adventure. After she returned from Mount Perry Florence flew from Sydney to Alice Springs, where she hired a truck 'weighted with oil drums to keep the vehicle on the road' before she 'bumped her way over corrugated roads fifteen inches (about 38 centimetres) thick with dust'. Drawing on bush skills she had picked up from her father, Florence washed herself and her clothes in creeks, cooked over a campfire and slept under the stars.

Her days were spent rattling along bush tracks in search of things to paint. When she located a scene worthy of her attention, Florence parked the truck in the shade, took out a giant beach umbrella and her palette of paints and set to work capturing the last light of the sun in purple and red streaks across the sky, the vivid red soil of the desert, the hazy outline of distant mountains at dusk or the sandstone outcrops that change colour as the morning creeps away. It was on this trip that Florence painted a dramatic, sweeping view of the MacDonnell Ranges. According to Florence this painting was commissioned by Sir Winston Churchill and she claims she sent it to his address in London. 'Sir Winston told me he prizes it very highly,' she remarked cheekily.

When she returned to Sydney, Florence unashamedly used her adventures in the outback as a promotional tool for her impending exhibitions. In one press interview she said, 'It's a risk for a woman to go alone in the desert, but I've been lucky. I haven't had an accident with the car, the spiders here aren't very dangerous and the snakes never seem to attack me. The birds are very friendly. When I sit down and start painting, they soon see I'm not going to harm them, and they come closer.' Another article reported the following: 'Miss Broadhurst, who paints under her maiden name, spends much of her time travelling in the outback . . . She sketches and paints wherever she goes' (*Australia Magazine*, 1954).

The David Jones Art Gallery on Elizabeth Street, Sydney, provided the scene for Florence's first solo exhi-

bition called 'Paintings of Australia'. Launched on 19 May
1954, over one hundred of her paintings filled three rooms.
Among the images of beaches, deserts, streetscapes, buildings, landscapes, animals, people and plants, one of the
main attractions was the sizeable canvas of Mount Perry's
Grand Hotel. Sydney art critics hailed her work as ' . . .
alive, dynamic and vital. An astonishing effort . . . her
statements are rhapsodical manifestoes, relying on a rich
impasto for much of their force . . .' and ' . . . the artist
favours bold patterns, and exploits colour gradations . . .
her robust approach accentuates every mood . . .' Other
reporters were less than impressed. This review was
published in the *Sydney Morning Herald* on the same day
as her exhibition opened:

> The paintings of Florence Broadhurst have been hiber-
> nating in quite a different climate. In this big exhibition
> of 108 works at David Jones' Art Gallery, the past is
> recalled in a beautiful technicolour dream. In fact,
> 'beauty' is very much in evidence, even when such
> titles as 'Opal beauty of the Reef' or 'Scorched Beauty'
> do not support the idea among other works . . . Miss
> Broadhurst is undoubtedly fond of the Australian land-
> scape, a sentiment to be applauded. Yet her gifts are
> insufficient to lend emphasis to that love. One cannot
> help but feel that she does not understand the true

Florence atop a camel on one of her many adventures through the East in the twenties.

COLLECTION: POWERHOUSE MUSEUM, SYDNEY, AUSTRALIA.

On 22 June 1929, Florence married Percy Walter Gladstone Kann at the Church of the Immaculate Heart of St Mary in South Kensington, London. It is probable that this photograph was taken at the nearby Kensington Gardens.

COLLECTION: POWERHOUSE MUSEUM, SYDNEY, AUSTRALIA.

FLORENCE BROADHURST traces a wallpaper design in her Crows Nest studio while assistant **JOHN LANG** makes a print from another.

Florence at her Australian (Hand Printed) Wallpaper company headquarters in Sydney's Crows Nest with her assistant, John Lang, in the early-sixties.

An interior shot of the Crows Nest wallpaper business that was launched in 1959. Florence peruses her design at the head of one of the many 14-metre-long printing tables.

She paints for at least six hours a day in the studio attached to her Manly (Sydney) flat. "By 7 a.m. I am bathed and ready to paint," she says. "I used to be a concert singer, but now I prefer painting .to singing. It's one of the sister arts, you know," she adds.

The artist Florence Broadhurst painting at her easel in her Manly flat in 1954. Florence was confident enough with her talent to remark that Australia had 'never before been properly shown on canvas. My oil paintings give a new angle on Australia.' This image featured in an article aptly titled 'Ambassadress with a paintbrush', in the mid-fifties.

FLORENCE BROADHURST talks with one of the truck drivers of her fleet, **TONY HEFFERNON,** over the bonnet of a "seven-tonner."

Florence chats to one of the many truck drivers in her employ at L. Lewis and Son, a Crows Nest based trucking company that she and her second husband, Leonard Lloyd Lewis, launched in 1959. Taking Florence seriously would have been a minor feat for some of the staff in her employ; their boss turned up to the truck yard in lurex mini-skirts, beehives and mink coats.

A spread from Australian Home Journal.

Main photo: Florence at the entrance of her Australian (Hand Printed) Wallpaper studio in Crows Nest with her chief assistant, Cathy Isimus.

Small photos (left to right):

1. *Cathy copies the prototype of a wallpaper design onto a silk screen.*
2. *Next, Cathy colours the pattern onto a screen.*
3. *The pattern is printed onto wallpaper by brushing the upper surface of the screen (it is probable that this staff member is David Bond, Florence's head printer).*
4. *The air is fanned above the final product to help it dry.*
5. *One of Florence's workers scrubs the silk screen clean.*

the
paper maker

IF you feel that the age we are living in is fa automated and uniform, then be thankful for the Flo Broadhursts of this world. Bubbling with enthusias new ideas and sheer love of life, Florence Broa has turned her unbounded energies to making printed wallpapers in a simple factory in a S suburb.

As far as we can tell, she is the only person in tralia to do this. Originally from Sussex, England, she learned her art, Miss Broadhurst does her des among the stacks and piles of wallpapers and fi designs stretched on racks to dry with girls fanni air above them. The papers and colors she us specially imported from abroad; the papers from S and the colors from all over the world. These form basis of Miss Broadhurst's collection, but before really satisfied with a shade she usually mixes the herself.

"I was once asked to print a carpet," she said. " three months' research, and I had to get all the from the Orient to get the right shades."

All the technical aids for the production of printed wallpapers Miss Broadhurst has improvised — drying racks, paint-mixing machines, and apparatus. It is because of this unique treatment th Broadhurst's papers are so individual.

"You get so involved with art that you lose t time," said Miss Broadhurst. "And I'm sure there be no psychiatric wards if there was more art. Peo take LSD must be terribly bored. I don't need it the more I do the more I can cope with.

"I haven't had a holiday in seven years, but I switch off when I want to. I was once asked. 'How know you are living?' and I said, 'I create, so I am living.' "

Miss Broadhurst designs to order, though sh some standard designs always in stock, and they a added to every year as she gets new ideas furnishing fashions change. "You have to keep a c balanced," she said. The detail and color of Broadhurst's work is really amazin . She has ev from the most fantastic psychedelic patterns and the most traditional designs.

(Florence Broadhurst wallpapers are available fr Pacific Highway (behind the boatshed), Crov N.S.W., or from Sydney decorators' shops.)

STORY/PENELOPE ROGERS, PICTURES/RODNEY WEI

1. Cathy Asimus, Miss Broadhurst's chief assistant, i up a prototype of a pattern ready for reproducing screen. 2. Cathy then colors the pattern on to the scree pattern is printed on to the wallpaper by brushing surface of the screen. 4. On particularly humid d the air is very still, the air must be disturbed above to aid the drying process. 5. Silk screen is being scrubl

FLORENCE BROAD
SCHOOL OF DE

A striking image of Florence in the upstairs showroom of her studio-factory on Royalston Street in Paddington. When she moved to these new premises in 1969, she also changed the name of the company from Australian (Hand Printed) Wallpapers to Florence Broadhurst Wallpapers. It hailed a new era of success for the flamboyant redhead.

character of the landscapes she paints, that her eye, indeed, only devours surface beauties, skin deep at best, without realising the structure beneath. Here, above all, a case can be made out for further study in the very rudiments of painting, even if only to strengthen the vague ideas in 'Scorched Beauty', 'Summer Rhapsody', 'The Swamp' or 'Sub-tropical Beauty', when Opus 109 sees the light of day.

Despite the potentially damaging nature of this bad review, it did little to affect Florence. When 'Paintings of Australia' featured at Finney's Art Gallery in Brisbane later the same year, a reporter from the *Canberra Times* claimed the launch of the show 'set record attendance figures'.

The stir that Florence caused in the press meant that both the Sydney and the Brisbane exhibitions sold out and she had no work left to take to England to 'encourage more British migrants' to come to Australia. Later she exhibited her work with an 'Australiana' theme at Anthony Hordern & Sons Art Gallery in Sydney and the Masonic Hall in Bathurst. She also arranged for a representative from the British Arts Council to launch (and add credence to) her large exhibition in Canberra.

Florence was soon involved in collaborative exhibitions with other Australian artists of note. The All Nations Club, on Bayswater Road in Kings Cross, was the venue for the Ten Guinea show that was launched on 12 October 1954. Florence's painting *Autumn Trees, Orange* featured alongside Australian artists including Roland Wakelin (who painted a moody evening scene at Double Bay), Judy Cassab and James Gleeson. A positive response from critics and the public alike soon prompted Florence to submit her work to the prestigious Archibald, Wynne and Sulman prizes. Her submission to the 1961 Archibald Prize was a very vibrant, yet sad and reflective, self-portrait. It is now part of the collection at the State Library in Sydney. The Queensland Art Gallery also acquired one of Florence's landscape paintings called *Wind of the South* which they paid 25 guineas for on 3 August 1954. It is now insured for two thousand dollars. As the title suggests, the oil on a canvas composition board painting features a windswept landscape that looks like a quintessential south coast of New South Wales beach scene. It comprises a tangle of grassy tussocks on a sandy knoll with the sea and sky on the distant horizon. Other information accessed from the Queensland Art Gallery also suggests that Florence entered some of her oil paintings into the H.C. Richards Memorial Prize for Painting in 1954 (*Temporary Defeat*) and 1955 (Untitled). The remainder of her work now exists in family and private collections. A small portion of these consist of the thirty-one paintings that Robert sent to auction after her death in 1981.

•

Art might imitate life but is never life itself. Florence needed other outlets. Soon, after all this success with her painting, Florence was in demand on the public speaking circuit. It was not the first time that she had stood in front of a crowd at the pulpit. She was first introduced to public speaking while living in London in the thirties, when she was a voluntary speaker for the Women-for-Westminster Movement and a member of the Conservative Party's panel of speakers (through which Florence said she met and befriended Sir Winston Churchill).

In London and in Sydney Florence gave impassioned lectures on art, business and the place of women in world affairs. She delivered her speeches with passion, vigour and eloquence. Just as Florence had once admired (and modelled herself on) entertainers such as Gladys Moncrieff and Dame Clara Butt, her new exemplaries were thinkers, writers and public speakers, among them people like Winston Churchill, Lady Ravensdale and Ethel Mannin.

Florence's lectures were often peppered with pompous Churchillian-style phrases such as, 'There are men whose manners have the same essential brilliance as the ancient Greeks' and 'All of us can figuratively look out on a world . . . and watch with clearer eyes the personalities and trends and events which in the aggregate constitute the cavalcade of contemporary history'.

Never missing an opportunity to use these many social events to her advantage, her lectures (at the Royal Empire Society, the Voice, Interests and Education of Women's Club, the United Nations Association of Australia and the Australian Society for Medical Research to name a few) were always accompanied by the donation of one of her paintings. Florence became even cleverer at promoting her work by infiltrating Sydney's social set, serving on charity committees, arranging décor for balls and being chums with socialites such as Jill Wran, Pattie Menzies, Jeannie Little and Lady Sonia McMahon, who naturally asked for her decorating advice. She devoted herself to a number of charities including the Royal Art Society of New South Wales, the YWCA, the Elizabethan Theatre Trust and the New South Wales Rotary Clubs. Though her long list of charity contributions looks impressive, Ria Murch, who worked with Florence at an Australian Red Cross Society op-shop on Market Street in Sydney, was dismissive of her contribution: 'She was a bloody nuisance who didn't know the first thing about working in an op-shop. She flitted about like a bloody butterfly.'

Florence had bigger and better fundraising ideas than op-shops, fetes and crocheted doilies. In 1957, she organised a competition (in association with the International

Ball Committee and the United Nations Association) to find a national costume for the men and women of Australia. Two hundred entrants battled for the prize of a holiday to Lord Howe Island and the chance to parade their design at the glitzy art deco nightclub The Trocadero, located on George Street, Sydney. A bank clerk from Mosman and a professional artist from Wentworthville were the winners. For the Sheilas there was an olive dress with a trim of wattle-inspired patterns and a wide-brimmed sun hat; and for the Bruces there were moleskin trousers tucked into leather boots and a gold shirt with a green neck tie. As a reporter remarked at the time:

> We've had to wait for an Englishwoman to sense the need for a new symbol of the warratah and wattle spirit with which Henry Lawson and his contemporaries stirred our somewhat lethargic embers of patriotism 50 years ago. This time, instead of a poet, it's an artist—Florence Broadhurst—who has started the crusade.

Though it was Florence who kick-started the concept for the competition, Phyllis Shillito took time out from her teaching post at the East Sydney Technical College to help Florence judge the entries. Florence could not have had a better assistant. Phyllis (who later established and ran the Shillito Design School in Sydney from 1962–80) is widely regarded as a crucial player in the advancement of Australian design.

But it was at a charity preview of the MGM movie *Dunkirk*, that Florence really made a splash on Sydney's social scene. The 1958 film starred Bernard Lee, John Mills and Richard Attenborough and screened at the St James Theatre. It was preceeded by a cocktail party at the Forum Club. Leonard Lloyd Lewis recalled the event, organised by his wife, who was by this stage the president of the Red Cross Ball Committee: 'The house was packed and before the preview Florence made a speech. She was superbly gowned. She literally shimmered. When she had finished, the Governor-General, Sir William Slim, dug me in the side with his elbow during the thunderous applause and said, "Absolutely wonderful. That's the most Churchillian speech I've ever heard." For me it was a crowning moment and a very apt description of Florence. She was Churchillian in outlook. She had a completely undaunted spirit' (*Australian Women's Weekly*, 1977).

To coincide with the event, the commissioning editor of the *Daily Mirror* asked Florence, to pen an article that reflected her personal experiences of World War II. The article was published on 10 July 1958:

I shall never forget the feeling that swept through England. The fact that 90 000 men were taken off the beaches in 700 craft, of all types, was nothing short of a miracle—it was divine intervention that the Channel should be calm enough for them to make the crossing, and that the Luftwaffe shouldn't bomb them into extinction. For the men and women who helped achieve that glorious retreat it was, I believe, the greatest moment of their lives, an opportunity to carry the torch of freedom. If we had surrendered then we would have lost the freedom of the world— it was the turning point of the war. Now it has become a memorial of Britain's hour of greatness. The miracle of Dunkirk was such a source of inspiration that the whole atmosphere in England changed—men worked in factories till they dropped. I saw them under their machines where they'd fallen asleep and couldn't work another minute. Bombs fell, people were killed but nobody complained—they'd got the will to go on.

Florence, who had by now gained a reputation for embellishing the truth, also exaggerated her time living on the poverty line: 'My impending blindness is due to the war. A lack of vitamins in my diet apparently created the condition. I'm not alone in this—thousands of English people have suffered the same way—thirteen years was a long time without proper food.'

And true to form, Florence didn't miss the opportunity to use the newspaper article to promote her work:

When the *Dunkirk* premiere is over (and the International Ball, for which I've been working also) I'm going back to my painting . . . I've been away from painting for a year and I've missed it terribly. Now I'm going on with my collection of Australiana, while I can. When I have 100 paintings together, I shall hold exhibitions in London, Paris and New York. I shan't be able to go outdoors, the sunlight is far too strong and the distances too great for me to see to paint the wonderful bizarre colours of Australia's scenery. I shall paint that great outdoors in my studio from memory with what sight I have left.

●

At fifty-eight years of age, Florence's failing eyesight did little to quell her appetite for wild colours. On the contrary, her inability to see as well as she used to (combined with her stubborn refusal to accept her doctor's advice to slow down), fuelled Florence's passion for anything bigger, bolder and brighter. She dyed her hair pink and wore outfits that were completely over the top. The Florence that actress and author Kate Fitzpatrick remembered wore false eyelashes that were dyed red to match the colour of her hair: 'I'm not sure where she got them, I've never seen them since, but they were nothing short of absolutely startling.' Her sister, Sally Fitzpatrick, who worked for Florence from 1967 until 1970, remembered being called upon to stick the false eyelashes on Florence once or twice a week:

When the clock struck five o'clock on Friday afternoon, Florence would pull out her lashes and I'd have to glue them on. By the time she arrived back at work on Monday morning, after a wild, boozy weekend, she would have just have a few stray strands hanging on for all they were worth to the middle of her upper eyelid. It was absolutely hilarious. Flo would waltz into the studio from her wild weekend and say, 'Oh fabulous, fabulous darling. I've had the most fabulous time partying. Would you mind fixing up my eyes?' Then I'd have to paste some fresh, new red falsies on until she was due for another change on Friday.

When Sally first met Florence, her boss was wearing a multi-coloured mu-mu, orange stilettos with heels that had worn away, bright plexi-glass rings on one hand and massive carat diamonds on the other. 'She had her bum in the air, her panties down to her knees and she was throwing rolls of wallpaper through her legs. She was crazy and fabulous.'

At one event in the mid-sixites, Florence turned up in a vibrant plum kaftan, with lashings of green eye shadow, bright orange lipstick and lurid yellow stockings. At another she wore a classic black Christian Dior frock with large white orchids pinned to her lapel and a velvet hat sprinkled with red diamantes.

Wherever Florence went, the Sydney press reported it and the vibrant socialite made sure she looked the part. As one reporter said, 'Her artist's brush and colour sense has "gone to the head" of well known personality Florence Broadhurst. Florence entered Romano's yesterday with a distinct tint of pink in her hair. She wore a black wool sack, draped at the back, high fashion black shoes with gold tips, and set the outfit off with grey mink.' And another described her as being '. . . like a painted red-headed butterfly emerging from a purple chiffon cocoon—always colourful Florence Broadhurst . . .' Florence not only enjoyed the attention lavished upon her by the press, she courted it. The 'English artist' soon became a regular in the social pages with a style reminiscent of Bette Davis, Gloria Swanson and Audrey Hepburn with a zany, theatrical twist. Florence was high camp.

Many of the charities that Florence associated herself with also had an artistic bent. She was responsible for the décor for society balls and specialised in fitting out the interiors. As if by magic she transformed drab, conservative rooms into exotic, glittering labyrinths. When she was given the job of organising the décor for a fundraiser for the Opera House in 1964 the result was a veritable kaleidoscope of colour: 'Shimmering blues, exciting crimsons, cloths of gold, sequins in the colours of the rainbow. The décor had an out-of-this-world charm. Artist Florence Broadhurst designed it and she had a top-drawer team of helpers who worked all through the day pinning dreamy, coloured butterflies on fairy festoons of black net. What a background for your new ball gown!' (*Sunday Mirror*, 1964). In a very short time, Florence had stamped her style on events all over Sydney.

•

In February 1958, when the Queen Mother visited Australia, Florence received not one but two invitations to join the visiting royal at gala events in Sydney—a reception for women at The Trocadero and, the following day, a garden luncheon at Government House. At the former event on George Street, a staggering eight hundred women representing one hundred and fifty different charity organisations, packed into the venue to catch a glimpse of the

Queen Mother. On the street was one of the wildest scenes of the royal tour. As British flags fluttered in the breeze overhead, two thousand near-hysterical women tried to force their way into the building. But they were no match for the police who held them back as a dignified Queen Mother alighted from the royal car and trotted through the front doors of the art deco dance hall.

Wearing her customary toque, pearls and a white organza dress, the Queen Mother gave a little wave as she made her way past the doormen dressed in smart red uniforms. The elegant royal walked the length of the scarlet carpet, covered with a pattern of fleur-de-lis picked out in cream and black, across the dance floor with a brass band behind her on the stage, before spotting Florence in the crowd. According to the *Daily Telegraph*, the Queen Mother walked over to Florence, who must have stood out like a beacon with her bright pink hair, and asked simply, 'Are you living here now?'

A few days later, on 26 February 1958, hundreds of guests, including Florence and Leonard, gathered on the lawns of Sydney's Government House awaiting the arrival of the Queen Mother. A luncheon had been organised in her honour and the place was abuzz with women in hats, gloves and conservative frocks cropped at mid-calf. The men wore either full military regalia or dashing three-piece suits with highly polished shoes.

Just the day before, many of these well-dressed guests would have seen the headlines emblazoned across page thirty-two of the *Daily Telegraph*: 'Queen Mother Renewed Old Acquaintance'. The article continued: 'Alert as ever, the Queen Mother was quick to recognise an old acquaintance yesterday, when she attended the Women's Reception at The Trocadero. The lucky person who caught Her Majesty's eye was artist Florence Broadhurst. "Are you living here now?" the Queen Mother asked Miss Broadhurst, who left England nine years ago.' The article continued, explaining that the British dignitary first met the redheaded Queenslander in 1947 when her daughter Queen Elizabeth married Philip Mountbatten and 'they had spoken several times since on different occasions'. Many of the guests who attended the luncheon at Government House would have been slightly envious, or at least curious. How had Florence managed to score an invitation to one of the hottest events in post-war Britain? Which of the royals was Florence chummy with—the Queen, her mother or both? And what was Queen Elizabeth's wedding frock *really* like?

As the guests at Government House mingled under the cloudless summer sky, the Queen Mother's car inched its way along congested Sydney streets lined with over a million fans. In Market Street, between Pyrmont Bridge and St James Station, one hundred thousand people jostled each other on the hot footpath just to catch a glimpse of her. A dozen times members of the crowd carrying gifts for the royal matriarch rushed onto the road and mobbed the car. When making progress became almost impossible, the Queen Mother ordered the car to stop while she graciously accepted bouquets and trinkets from her adoring public.

At Government House Governor Lieutenant General Sir Eric Woodward and his guests waited patiently for their guest and Florence kept them entertained with tales about the royal wedding. Her account of the event included details about the four-course breakfast that she and Leonard had enjoyed at Buckingham Palace. As Florence explained, she and her husband mingled with foreign royalty as they ate lavish fare that included the aptly named Filet de Sole Mountbatten and Bombe Glace Princesse Elizabeth. An elaborate procession followed their champagne-laden meal. From the palace, Florence claimed, she and the other guests travelled in coaches to Westminster Abbey while the Household Cavalry provided a mounted escort. Princess Elizabeth, dressed in her lustrous satin wedding dress embroidered with pearls and crystals, travelled behind them with her father, King George VI, in the Irish State Coach. When the future Queen of England arrived at Westminster Abbey her fifteen-foot train, held in place by a tiara of pearls and diamonds, dropped to the ground as she stepped from the coach and it followed her like a shadow into the church. The women attending the function at Government House would have listened to Florence in wide-eyed awe. By the time the Queen Mother finally arrived, Florence would have had her audience eating out of the palm of her hand.

But the story was a fabrication. The closest Florence got to Princess Elizabeth's wedding in 1947 were the ingredients donated by the Australian Girl Guides for the wedding cake. The reason Florence was acquainted with the Queen Mother was because she sold her a few frocks at Pellier Ltd—her Mayfair dress salon.

WALLPAPER AND TRUCKING

1959–1969

'I'm sure there would be no psychiatric wards if there was more art. People who take LSD must be terribly bored. I don't need it'

FLORENCE BROADHURST, 'THE PAPER MAKERS',
AUSTRALIAN HOME JOURNAL, 1968

The Lloyd Lewises had come a long way since they first arrived in Sydney from war-torn Europe in 1949. By 1958 they were wealthy, successful and well-connected on the Sydney social circuit. Everything had worked out as Florence had planned. She had carved a career for herself as a successful artist and continued to paint prolifically and exhibit often; her husband had made a success of himself as a financier, and her son, who was now twenty years old, had grown up in the healthy, abundant environment that she had always hoped for. As Florence explained to the *Daily Telegraph* in 1954: 'For me Australia is the promised land. I came here run-down, tired and war weary—the sunshine was a cure in itself and I never turned back. My son, who was pale and under-sized for his age, is now six foot one and thirteen stone.'

The enterprising couple owned by this time a number of investment properties around Sydney, but their home was a modern Potts Point penthouse on Macleay Street that cost them almost seven thousand pounds. The lavish split-level apartment was small but had a stunning bird's-eye view of the glittering Sydney Harbour. From their main bedroom and dining room on the upper level, they could watch boats sail past by day and lights shimmer across the waters of the harbour at night. The main bedroom was bursting with Florence's gowns, jewellery and makeup. It was a relatively sparse, monochromatic bedroom, except for dramatic floor-to-ceiling mirrors in which Florence preened herself every morning and evening. The lower level of the apartment featured a living room and a small kitchen that, as regular visitor Jeanette Moseley explained, was 'barely big enough to cook a chop'. Both rooms had views over a bustling Macleay Street.

Coincidentally, Ralph Sawyer, an old friend of Florence's from her Shanghai days, lived nearby. Ralph, the effeminate, slight (he only stood about 163 centimetres) and extremely convincing female impersonator, had not been as successful as Florence Broadhurst. When he first returned to Australia from Shanghai in 1941, he worked as a clerk in the public service and was later self-employed in a series of small businesses, including cafés, sandwich shops and rooming houses. Now he rented out rooms in his Macleay Street home to pay for his keep and managed an Elizabethan-style inn and restaurant on Elizabeth Bay Road which was, according to researcher Tony Barker, perpetually filled with theatrical, flamboyant and colourful characters. Tony remembers that Ralph later moved to Double Bay and then to the nearby suburb of Woollahra, where it was probable that Ralph and Florence bumped into each other. It is Ralph's Woollahra address that features in Florence's address book from this period. She had also added him to the invite list for her art exhibitions at about this time.

Life in the eastern suburbs of Sydney suited Florence. All her favourite haunts were within arm's reach: among them the Chevron Hilton Hotel, Napoleon's Café and an assortment of European-style boutiques. Judy Korner, whose family beauty salon was located at the Kings Cross Chevron Hilton throughout the sixties, said Florence was a regular customer. 'She came every week and got the lot done—facials, waxing, massage—you name it. She came in like a tornado and left like a tornado. She loved to be pampered. She moved with incredible speed. She projected an image of someone who was not to be messed with. She clicked her fingers and people jumped.' Judy claimed that Florence could often be found with Leonard or with

a friend at the hotel bar or listening to live acts such as
Shirley Bassey, Nat King Cole and Jose Feliciano.

•

Florence and Leonard were soon sketching out their idea
for a new endeavour, something that would make money
and was easy to manage. With Leonard's experience as a
diesel engineer and Florence's managerial nous, a motor
yard seemed like the perfect venture. In 1959 the husband-
and-wife team paid twenty thousand pounds for an old
truck yard at 466 Pacific Highway, Crows Nest. They took
down the old signs and erected new glossy ones which
read: L. Lewis and Son. The company earned its bread
and butter couriering goods interstate and buying and
selling new and used vehicles and machinery including
cars, trucks, semi-trailers and earth-moving equipment.
Toward the rear of the site, a collection of leaky sheds
and workshops were rented out to small businesses.

Florence and Leonard kick-started their scheme by
purchasing two scarlet seven-tonne trucks and set them
to work couriering goods back and forth to Brisbane.
When the trucks weren't on the road, they were parked
proudly in the dirt yard that fronted the Pacific Highway,
passed by trams, cars and buses at all hours. Emblazoned
on each truck door was a domed company crest.

It was a modest start, but it wasn't long before the venture, nudged along by Florence's tireless work ethic, started to grow. Soon the Lloyd Lewises bought out a Brisbane trucking company and added another six trucks to their fleet. With the rapid expansion of the business, the position of manager of the Brisbane office became available and Robert Lloyd Lewis was the perfect candidate. Since he had left Barker College in 1954 he had worked in a variety of jobs, but he was a natural with diesel engines. At twenty-one Robert moved north to Brisbane. By 1963, L. Lewis and Son was sailing along with a fleet of drivers, a sales manager and six assistants.

Set against a background of petrol, sweat and swearing, Florence had an otherworldly appearance as she waltzed around the Crows Nest truck yard with her flame-red beehive and lurex mini-skirts. Taking her seriously was a minor feat for some of the truck drivers and assistants in her employ, but the moment she opened her mouth it didn't take them long to work out who was the boss. Florence was brusque, direct and driven. She barked orders at her drivers and rapped them across the knuckles if they didn't do a good job. As Florence herself said:

Making money is hard. It calls for qualities of courage, resource and intelligence of a far higher order than is necessary to gain a university degree. It isn't your

position that holds you back, but your disposition.
Money is a means to an end, not an end in itself.

From her upstairs office she worked with vertiginous
speed as she juggled the endless round of details involved
in managing a rapidly expanding company. She organised cargo to be delivered and picked up, bought and sold
trucks, struck deals worth thousands of dollars, wrote and
signed contracts and kept her eye on her many invest-
ments dotted around Sydney.

The press found the duality of the colourful 'English'
artist who was also the managing director of a successful
trucking business hard to stomach. Consequently, Florence
became defensive about the perception the public might
have of her. As she declared to *People Magazine* in 1963,
'True artists don't boast they know nothing about practical matters, because that is admitting to a limited
mentality.' But the reporters did agree on one thing:
Florence was doing a good job. As one explained, 'Her
success in buying and selling motor vehicles is due, she
thinks, to an ability which proved just as profitable in a
millinery business she once ran in England—an ability to
choose efficient offsiders and delegate authority to them.'
Or as Florence put it, 'I employ people who know their
jobs, and then as problems come up, I see that they're
channelled to the right person' (*People Magazine*, 1963).

While there was little doubt that Florence was a hard worker who delegated efficiently and effectively, one thing was obvious: she didn't like getting her hands soiled. According to Robert, 'My mother didn't get involved with the day-to-day dirty work at the truck yard. She'd say, "Darling I'm not going to pick anything up, it's dirty"'.

·

One afternoon, a young designer of textiles, wrapping paper and wallpaper appeared at the truck yard. He had an appointment to inspect an old panel-beating shop that the Lloyd Lewises had for lease. John Lang, a polite, petite man, had made the trek from Melbourne to Sydney in search of a better, more profitable life for himself and was looking for somewhere to set up his printing tables. One glance at the space Florence had to rent and John made up his mind to take it. He soon settled in and Florence took an interest in what he was doing. As John explained, she would often call in via the back stairs leading from her office. 'Florence would quiz me, "Who would want wallpapers in this godforsaken country?" I was rapidly beginning to think she'd stop me getting any work done,' he said. He soon discovered that Florence was an astute businesswoman with a keen eye for a potentially successful venture. Lang claimed Florence said to him, 'What would a little boy like you know about business? You haven't got the contacts.' And on yet another visit, as her interest escalated, 'This is so exciting my dear. This commodity could be marketed in a very social way.'

Peter Leis, who was employed by Florence in the late sixties, remembered this scenario differently: 'As John was floundering and unable to pay the rent, she took the reins.' Robert echoed this memory: 'With John at the helm his wallpaper business wasn't a great success. Anyway, he couldn't even afford to pay the rent that was due to my parents, so my mother simply stepped in and took over. They worked together for a short period but not for very long and John soon left altogether.'

The exact originators of the business Australian (Hand Printed) Wallpapers Pty Ltd, registered in 1959, might never be known. And Florence did not help clarify the issue. Her reports varied, including that she got the idea for designing wallpaper when the trend became fashion-able in house decorating again; that she learnt the craft in Sussex, England, where she told staff members that she had been born; and that her idea was born from frustration as it was impossible to purchase interior decor-ations to suit her needs. On another occasion she claimed she got into designing wallpaper because she was sick of waiting for interior design products from overseas; and to the *Sun*, in 1962, she said she launched the venture because friends 'complained they walked the city without being able to find the exact colours they wanted'.

Either way, armed with her sharp business acumen, a penchant for work and a passion for vibrant colours, Florence threw herself into the wallpaper business. With only a handful of prospective clients, she established herself as the only Australian producing screen-printed wallpapers. Florence now juggled managing the trucking business, running Australia's only wallpaper factory and maintaining her much-loved painting. As a journalist from *People Magazine* in 1963 put it, 'tall, vital Florence Broadhurst lives three lives'.

To squeeze everything into her day, Florence rose at 6 am and painted for two hours in her Potts Point penthouse before arriving at the truck yard at around 8.30 am. She spent the rest of her day juggling two worlds that were each other's polar opposites: trucks and wallpaper. She barely had time to eat. Her holidays were a thing of the past. Florence even worked on weekends. And when she returned home in the early evening she devoted what spare time she had to her new love of portraiture.

When Florence started her wallpaper business, she had only two printing tables (inherited from John Lang) and two assistants who helped her produce around twenty rolls of hand-printed paper a week. It wasn't long before three other employees joined the crew. As Florence commented to a journalist at the time, 'I employ five people in the factory, and I do the work of four myself, so we manage.'

To protect the paper from incessant leaks in the ceiling, Florence installed oversized beach umbrellas along the length of each printing table. It was underneath these makeshift awnings that Florence designed her bright, bold and striking work 'among the stacks and piles of wallpapers and finished designs stretched on racks to dry with girls fanning the air above them' (*Australian Home Journal*, 1968). A journalist from the *Australian* in 1968 described her workplace rather romantically as 'a frail white timber and glass ediface rising from a sea of geranium tubs behind a garage'. Despite having enthusiastic staff, eager to work and learn, Florence often complained there was 'no pool of labour' for her to rely upon. As she once said: 'Each new member of staff had to be thoroughly trained by me. Even so, I found that they need constant supervision.'

Twelve months after Florence first opened her doors for business she issued her first catalogue. As Florence explained in a speech called 'Personalisation Pays Off', which she delivered on the public speaking circuit, she had carefully analysed her target market: 'Who was I aiming to supply? In the beginning, not the lower income bracket—I was interested in the people who could appreciate an original article and who wanted something other than mass produced items,' she said. Her catalogues were released to a number of carefully selected interior design and architectural firms in Sydney and Melbourne. According to Florence, 'This step actually proved to be the best method of maintaining consistent sales, as the decorators and architects involved me with supplying restaurants, clubs and companies as well as private clients.' In February 1962, two years after her catalogue was issued, the Decorator Clinic in Grace Bros on Broadway hosted a display of Florence Broadhurst wallpapers. The colours and designs of this exhibition summed up the mood and feel of the sixties: brave, garish and kitsch.

When Florence appeared on the Australian interior design scene it had (by international standards) just turned the corner from childhood into puberty. As late as the thirties, the majority of interior design hardware was being imported from abroad, while in the fifties many Australians were still living in dark, stuffy homes that were not conducive to the antipodean environment. The fifties and sixties marked a time when the pioneering work of organisations such as the Contemporary Art Society, the Commercial and Industrial Artists Association, the Design and Industries Association and the Society of Designers for Industry, which did much to promote the awareness and appreciation of design in Australia, started to pay dividends. Designers of note who made their mark on the new style that started to emerge at this time included acclaimed industrial designer Gordon Andrews, who not only designed Australia's new decimal currency notes of 1966, but created furniture and interiors for the New South Wales Government Tourist Bureau and the Australian Trade Commission; the multi-talented Max Forbes, who among other things designed the exhibition display for the 1956 Industrial and Graphic Design Exhibition that was part of the Melbourne Olympic Games Arts Festival and is considered to be Australia's first substantial design survey; graphic designer, painter and industrial designer of note, Alistair Morrison, otherwise known as Professor Afferbeck Lauder, the author of the book that defined the wonderful language of 'Strine'; Douglas Annand, who designed publicity material, textiles, murals and sculptures for companies such as Qantas, David Jones, P&O Orient Line, CSR and Shell; Anne Outlaw and Alexandra (Nan) Mackenzie, the creative founders of the Sydney-based Annan Fabrics—not to be confused with Douglas Annand—who landed a plethora of prestigious commissions and exhibited around the world; Clement Meadmore, now an internationally revered sculptor based in New York; furniture designers Fred Ward, Grant Featherston and Douglas Snelling; Woollahra-based interior designer, colourist and businesswoman Marion

Hall Best, who introduced many Australians to innovative furniture produced by world-class designers such as Eero Saarinen, Isamu Noguchi, Harry Bertoia and bold fabrics from Finland's Marimekko; and fabric designer and artist Frances Burke, who was a founding member of the Society of Industrial Designers Foundation and the Industrial Design Institute of Australia (now the Design Institute of Australia). It is a list that would not be complete without the mention of two other Australians who don't strictly fall into the realm of design. They include Martin Sharp, arguably Australia's most prominent popular artist, who first came to public attention in the early sixties for his cartoons in *Oz*, a satirical street magazine, and who later produced a host of internationally recognised posters, prints and record covers; and architect Harry Seidler, arguably Australia's leading architect of the modern movement, who has done much to change the perception of design in Australia and is the first architect in Australia to completely express the principles of the Bauhaus.

Even though Florence found herself in extremely good company, she swiftly made an ascent and found her niche in Australia's blossoming design industry. Anne-Marie Van de Ven, the curator of decorative arts and design from the Powerhouse Museum, claims that what differentiated Florence from her contemporaries was that Florence's venture was unique: 'Australian (Hand Printed) Wallpaper was unashamedly global in both its sources of inspiration and its marketing focus.' But it was not, as Florence often boasted, the first and only wallpaper factory in the southern hemisphere. Since the mid-nineteenth century, Australia had produced a swag of wallpaper manufacturers that included Melbourne's William Gutheridge, circa 1851; Charles Carter, who exhibited his work in the mid-1860s and who specialised in 'royal stamped burnished gold paper hangings of his own design'; the Painters and Paperhangers' Society of Victoria, that served as an early mediator for home grown and imported wallpaper in the late nineteenth century; Adelaide's J.W. Williams and Sydney's Gilkes & Co., who incorporated Australian motifs into their papers; and Morrison's, which was based on George Street, Sydney, in the twenties, who offered 'hand made Borders, Friezes and Wall Decorations . . . printed and designed in Australia'. These early papers ranged from conservative prints that were 'light cheerful patterns, well covered, not particularly "showy"— the neater and smaller the pattern the better' (Murphy, P. 1996); friezes that depicted landscapes and historical scenes; stylised art nouveau motifs such as roses and tulips; and elaborate ornamentation that combined ceiling papers, borders, friezes and stencilling all in the same room towards the end of the nineteenth century, when Australians were feeling a little braver.

Florence now had a new mission. Her desire was to 'cure people who display symptoms of the timid decorator syndrome. You spot them easily. They're always afraid of bold design and bright colour. When you suggest a perfectly suitable paper, they shy away with the same old excuses . . . "Oh but my kitchen's much too small for that!" or "Heavens! If I put that up I'd have spots before my eyes"' (*Australian*, 1968). As Florence said in an article aptly titled, 'We are now not so nervous of colour', which featured in the *Sydney Morning Herald* on 20 May 1966, 'You can state your character by your choice of wallpaper.' As Florence saw things, Australians were afraid of colour, preferring monochromatic tones that she believed were not vigorous enough to withstand modern living. 'Many [Australians] still think of wallpaper as something drab that grandmother had on the wall,' she said in the same article. Florence made it her business to change that perception.

By 1963, four years after the business commenced, the demand for Florence Broadhurst's wallpaper spiralled out of control. It was at this time that the tables, the rolls, the screens and the pots of paint outgrew the 'frail white edifice' and Florence arranged for an annex to be added to the building. She painted the ceiling of the extension in shimmering metallics and overlayed it with the first paper that she had ever designed: an off-white design sparsely dabbed with gold. On the floor, seven assistants battled to fill international orders. Gone were the days when Australian (Hand Printed) Wallpapers printed a meagre twenty rolls of paper a week. Now it pumped out two hundred rolls each week, with each roll taking around three weeks to prepare for printing. Ex-employee Ben Fitzpatrick remembered how tedious and time consuming the printing process was:

> Printing Flo's wallpapers was back-breaking work that was extremely complicated and time consuming. We spent eight hours a day bending over long printing tables, pulling the heavy squeegee manually over each screen, back and forth, trying to ensure that each layer of colour was applied correctly and matched up with the next roll. And because some of her designs had up to five or six colours in them, this seemed close to impossible at times, but somehow we managed to do it.

Ben, whose mother is acclaimed Australian artist and author Dawn Fitzpatrick and whose sister is actor and author Kate Fitzpatrick, claimed the design process was equally as arduous:

Because all of Flo's designs were done by hand, the designers had to sit down with a pen and a paintbrush and draw every single dot, every single stroke and every single minute detail. There were no printers or scanners to rely on back them; just manual labour, and a lot of time and commitment. To put it bluntly, it was an insane amount of work.

Ben's other sister Sally Fitzpatrick, who is now an artist based in the United States, also worked for Florence. Her forte was drawing and designing. She said:

I was fresh out of a convent school and I'd just shifted to Sydney. I was only seventeen years old when I went for my job interview at the Crows Nest shed. When I arrived at the studio Flo had another head designer, a young, perpetually drunk party girl who wasn't doing a very good job, and Flo asked me, 'Where's the portfolio of your drawings?' I replied that I didn't realise I had to bring one along, so Flo sent me home and said I had to come back with some evidence that I could draw. If she liked me, she'd pay me eighteen dollars a week; if she didn't I'd have to go. I spent the night putting some drawings together and when I went to see her the next day she accused me of tracing them, but she still gave me the job.

Once she could see I had the skill, she soon got rid of the party girl and I became her head designer. I was in tears every day for the next six months because Flo was so overwhelmingly powerful, but I continued to work for her for the next four years and we ended up being great friends. I adored her. She ended up being instrumental in moulding me in my youth. She showed me how to see a wilder, brighter world.

In 1963, there were now eighty designs in the Florence Broadhurst collection, including chaotic psychedelic swirls, orderly geometric patterns, Hellenic prints, Aztec symbols, exploding stars, mutating shapes, peacock feathers, fans, oriental filigree, bamboo, arabesques, art nouveau swirls, English florals, poppies, ferns with hatched fronds, blossoms, butterflies, storm clouds and quirky nursery prints. Some were masculine, tough and commanding, while others were feminine, soft and delicate. Like their creator, they were unique, arresting and ahead of their time. They packed a punch.

Much of the inspiration for these designs no doubt came from her travels through Asia and Europe, but it was when Florence arrived back in Australia in 1949 that she first experimented with bold, bright designs. Only one journalist who visited Florence's Manly studio in the fifties was astute enough to notice Florence's psychedelic

Florence, with a friend, at one of the lavish parties she frequently held at her Paddington studio-factory. Florence's parties were often themed, with dancers, bands and a glittering disco ball hanging from the ceiling.
MITCHELL LIBRARY, SLNSW.

In the late-sixties, Florence launched a new advertising campaign in a variety of magazines including Vogue Living*,* Australian House and Garden *and the* Australian Home Journal*. The advertisements claimed that Florence Broadhurst Wallpapers was 'the only studio of its kind in the world'. It also highlighted her prestigious international connections.*
MITCHELL LIBRARY, SLNSW.

The Lotus Bar in Sydney features a display of Florence Broadhurst wallpaper, providing a stylish backdrop to its modern interior.

The Tank Bar in Sydney also features a plethora of Florence Broadhurst wallpapers, in intimate booths that are reminiscent of thirties style.

Fashion designer Leona Edmiston's Sydney store has feature walls of Florence Broadhurst wallpaper in stunning metallics.

A handbag from the Funkis range of Florence Broadhurst paraphernalia that includes lampshades, cushion covers, fabric screens, upholstery fabric and bags.

COURTESY FUNKIS.

New Zealand-based fashion designer, Karen Walker, incorporated Florence's work into her 2001 and 2003 collections. This image features a trench coat from her 2001 'Pups' range which also included hoodies, T-shirts, singlets, jewellery, mini-skirts, buttons and bags.

COURTESY KAREN WALKER.

In 2001, and every year since, Sydney-based fashion design company, Zimmerman, have used Florence Broadhurst prints (blossoms, hibiscus flowers, lilies and the like) in their swimwear and clothing collections.

COURTESY ZIMMERMAN.

Sydney-based company Customweave Carpets and Rugs, gave Florence Broadhurst's work a new twist: in 2003, they launched a collection of rugs embossed with her bamboo, butterfly and Japanese-inspired floral work. The rugs are woven with a tactile mix of beads, leather, felt and wool.

In 2002, Melbourne-based designer Matthew Butler, of Bluesquare, came up with the novel concept of covering his angular Polar chairs with filmy lengths of Florence Broadhurst fabric. Matthew says the idea came after he saw Akira Isogawa dresses and he wanted to 'fuse fashion and furniture'.

Courtesy Bluesquare.

Fashion designer, Akira Isogawa, was one of the first modern designers to spot the potential of the Florence Broadhurst collection of prints. In his 2000 and 2002 collections, Akira featured jackets, skirts and dresses printed with Florence's designs in his Paris shows.

Courtesy Akira Isogawa.

Sydney-based designer, Greg Natale, created this tribute to Florence Broadhurst in 2002. Later that year, the design won a 'Wild Card' award in the 'Belle/Space Apartment of the Year' competition. Judges were so impressed—and bemused— they were forced to create a made-to fit category especially for the project. The apartment features an 'uber' matched look, dictated by Florence Broadhurst wallpaper in a palette of navy blue, beige and white.

Courtesy Greg Natale Interior Design.

paintings hidden among her Australian canvases. It is hard to imagine how they could be overlooked. The paintings were bursting with vibrant, graphic patterns and pre-empted the drug-induced psychedelia of the sixties. The journalist said, 'Besides her serious work you will see what amounts to mediumistic design . . . swirls and patterns which appear to come from the subconscious'.

Florence agreed that her work had a 'mediumistic' quality. She claimed to the journalist that her designs appeared in her mind at all hours of the day and night, and that she had so many creative ideas she could never keep up with them all. 'You get so involved with art you lose track of time . . . I'm sure there would be no psychiatric wards if there was more art. People who take LSD must be terribly bored. I don't need it' (*Australian Home Journal*, 1968).

Colour was Florence's forte. She made an exacting art out of mixing paint to match her clients' samples of carpet, upholstery fabrics, artwork and the like. Florence Broadhurst wallpaper could be printed in any colour or in any combination. 'I mix all the colour. Industrial chemists sometimes take three days to do this—I do it in three minutes! You're either a colourist or you're not,' she declared to the *Australian Women's Weekly* in 1965. Florence also did brisk business custom designing paper for clients who wanted something special or who were too far away to visit her in Crows Nest. Florence received swags of letters and from her headquarters she spun her intuitive magic and gave her correspondents' homes a makeover. As Florence explained, 'I've had orders from Thursday Island, Perth and New Zealand. A woman living way up in the Gulf of Carpentaria wrote and described her "room for entertaining"—I thought she must entertain crocs or something. They all write telling me about the room, where the windows are and such, and I design something to fit. I've never had anybody send it back yet.' By 1965 Florence claimed that she developed a new design every week. Her philosophy was to give people choice because as she put it, 'people want something to reject, don't they?' (*Australian Women's Weekly*, 1965).

What set Florence apart from her overseas competitors was that her wallpaper designs could not be cut from the old stencil method and that her custom-designed screens were a one-off. When a client collected their individually designed roll of paper, they also had the opportunity to collect the individually made screen. Florence was a perfectionist with a highly personalised business approach. Even though she employed a troupe of assistants that included David Bond, Florence's loyal head printer who remained with her from 1960 until the day she died in 1977, she still watched over every element of production, including design, screen-making and colour-mixing and printing. She worked closely with her employees and never missed a trick. As she explained to the *Sun* in 1962, 'I've found a team of young artists who have just completed their courses. I tell them what I want and then correct and make improvements to their work until we have the perfect design.' One of these artists was a thirty-year-old mother of two, Annie Georgeson.

In 1966, Annie spotted an advertisement for Florence Broadhurst wallpaper in a magazine. 'Basically I decided to give her a call and ask Florence whether I could come and learn the art of silkscreen printing from her,' Annie told me. She added:

> But as Florence explained, she didn't normally take students, but for some reason she decided to take me on. When I arrived at the tin shed at Crows Nest, she had taken on another student, an American woman, as well. As far as I'm aware we were the only students Florence Broadhurst ever had. Of course Florence had young artists in her employ, but Florence was paying these people. We never worked for her.

For the next year, Annie and 'the woman from America' frequented the tin shed in Crows Nest three days each week. Their days were filled with lessons on drawing up designs, amending designs, cutting stencils and printing.

'Florence was very encouraging of our work. We all got on well. She was a great innovator,' said Annie. Florence's students were allocated space and benches at one end of the shed and executed their work (which they later took home with them) in an environment that Annie describes as practical, unsophisticated, yet bustling with activity:

> Although Florence had a thousand other tasks to attend to, she still gave us the time of day. You got the feeling that David Bond, her head printer, who was like a permanent fixture at the truck yard, helped everything run more smoothly for Florence. He was like her anchor. He was competent at what he did and enjoyed it. They appeared to work well together. He was laid back, comfortable, friendly and she was like a volcano, a whirlwind. But though they worked well as a team, I remember thinking I'd rather be learning from her than working for her. She was extremely demanding. But I think she really needed David so she cut him some slack.

Ben Fitzpatrick agreed with Annie's assessment of the relationship between David and Florence: 'David was a dinky-di Aussie bloke who made Florence her money. He was a hard worker and Florence gave him a trade. What he did took real skill, he was a craftsman.' And according to Sally Fitzpatrick, 'Florence pulled David Bond off the streets. He was a boxer. He was a great guy and Florence saved him. He was with her from the beginning, right to the bitter end. I believe she loved him very much.'

Even though Florence had her hands full designing, printing and overseeing staff and students, she got a kick out of dealing directly with her clients and her wallpapers were not for sale on the wholesale market. As Florence put it in the *Australian* on 16 October 1968, 'I like dealing with people in person, and I want to keep the business to a size where this will always be possible.'

It was a savvy approach that meant her designs soon evolved into what her son Robert referred to as a 'status symbol'. Her clients felt that not only were they purchasing a unique product, but they were being well looked after. Though Florence Broadhurst wallpaper was an expensive interior design solution in the sixties, her clients were happy to pay. 'If [Florence's] papers seem expensive, varying from $8 to $30 a roll, it's because she claims to do by hand what can't be done by the most complex machinery.'

•

Success, however, made a failure of the Lloyd Lewis marriage. While Florence was busy building her latest business, Leonard, who once described his romance with

Florence as a 'young good looking man meeting a film star' was having an affair with a younger woman. Leonard's new mistress, Janice Marie Boulton, known by her nickname 'Cherry', was everything that Florence was not. While Florence was self-centred, strident and demanding, Cherry was selfless, gentle and easy-going. Leonard's divorce from Florence, after twenty-six years of marriage, was swift and he married 'Cherry' in Southport, Queensland, in 1961. Florence was devastated but, according to Leonard, forgiving. 'Florence treated my new wife like a daughter-in-law with love and affection . . . There was some bitterness when our marriage broke up, Florence was able to overcome it' (*Australian Woman's Weekly*, 16 November 1977). Nerida Greenwood, a former employee, gave a different version of events: 'Florence and her husband didn't really like each other very much. They were always dobbing each other in to the taxation office.' Sally Fitzpatrick claimed that Florence could not stand Leonard: 'Whenever he came near her, she'd scream and shout at him. She told me she'd set him up in two or three businesses and he'd run them all into the ground, including the trucking business. She said everything that he touched turned to rot.'

After his second marriage, Leonard left his home, his son, his business affairs and his life in Sydney and shifted with Cherry to Western Australia where they became involved in the art world. There they had two children, a daughter Roshana and a son David. To this day, Cherry and Roshana are still involved with art. In 1999, Roshana set up the Lister Calder Gallery located in Subiaco, Perth. The gallery exhibits modern Australian art by artists such as Arthur Boyd, Norman Lindsay, Albert Tucker, Brett Whiteley and Fred Williams.

After her divorce from Leonard, Florence kept her head high. Jeanette Mosely, whose portrait Florence painted in 1961, remembered this period vividly. 'Although Florence was an extremely glamorous woman in her prime and her husband dumped her for a younger woman, she wasn't shamed like most women in that era. She wanted to keep herself where she felt she belonged—on a pedestal.'

Jeanette and Florence met at a charity event in Sydney's east when Jeanette was a twenty-seven-year-old waitress, and Florence, who was in her sixties, was a highbrow guest. As the guests filed out at the end of the event, Florence approached Jeanette. 'She stuck out her gloved hand and announced abruptly, "I would like to paint you." We swapped details and I received a telephone call a week later. It was Florence. All she said was, "I need you tonight",' explained Jeanette. 'I was bemused by her abrupt manner, but I was extremely naïve and felt honoured that this grand dame of high society chose me as her subject.'

For the next eighteen months Jeanette spent one evening a week at Florence's penthouse apartment which she described as 'like fairyland, the height of glamour'. The arrangement was always the same: in the living room an easel and a chair faced each other in readiness for the painting session; the women didn't talk, except for idle chit chat, and when Jeanette arrived she headed straight for the bathroom, where she changed out of her work clothes into the scarlet jumper that featured in her portrait. In the bathroom, she was puzzled to see that the bathtub was filled to capacity with wreaths of flowers still in their wrappers. 'I'm not talking about a few wreaths, I'm talking about an entire bathtub literally overflowing with them and it wasn't just on the odd occasion, but every single week. All I could think of was that Florence had a lot of admirers,' she exclaimed. When Jeanette sat in the chair that faced the easel, there was no mention of the flowers in the bathtub or enquiries about how Jeanette had spent her week. As Jeanette explained:

She wasn't personable. She didn't connect with people. She kept everything close to her chest and didn't care about what the other person thought, felt or believed. Florence made people around her feel nervous and intimidated. Her eye contact was extremely intense and whenever she was around there was tension in the air. It was as if she was preoccupied or thinking deeply all the time.

Jeanette found the stony silence awkward while Florence painted. But one evening in 1961 was special. The revered Australian artist Joshua Smith caught the lift to Florence's apartment to watch Florence paint. It was 1944 when Smith hit the headlines after William Dobell painted a portrait of him for the Archibald portrait prize. When the painting won, the portrait was at the centre of intense opposition between the ancients and moderns in the New South Wales art world, when it was argued that the painting did not qualify as a portrait because it was in fact a caricature. The lengthy court case obtained wide publicity and evoked strong public opinion, and it affected Joshua's health and reputation.

Joshua, a talented artist in his own right, later painted a portrait of Florence sitting at her easel, which he entered into the Archibald Prize. On this evening Joshua perched beside Florence while she painted Jeanette. 'They just mumbled to each other all evening and every now and then he'd make a comment on her brushstroke,' claimed Jeanette. After Florence died, Jeanette tried to track down her youthful portrait and was dismayed to discover that Robert had auctioned it off along with many of his mother's other portrait paintings. Jeanette's portrait was one in a series that Florence was working on when she first met Jeanette. The other paintings were of people Florence met on the street such as a hairdresser, a deli owner, a florist, and a butcher. When the paintings were finished, Florence organised a party for her subjects in her apartment. According to Jeanette they all sat cross-legged on the floor around a bowl of Smiths Crisps and played marbles. 'It was boring, but I suppose Florence thought it was a novel idea. I went there expecting to meet someone famous or fabulous. I guess the other guests did too, but in the end we were just a bunch of locals that she had painted.'

Florence's friendship with Joshua Smith was an enduring one. There are claims that he accompanied Florence on some of her painting expeditions to Queensland in the fifties. Ted Bettiens thinks he met Joshua in Mount Perry. 'All that he and Florence wanted to talk about was the colour of the landscape and the colour of the soil and the sky,' he said. Sally Fitzpatrick recalled meeting Joshua in Florence's apartment in the late sixties:

I walked in and there was Florence with her easel set up and sitting beside her with his easel set up was Joshua Smith. The two of them were just sitting there in the dark, painting and knocking back cocktails. I didn't realise who it was at the time, but when she told me I was literally thunderstruck. That's when I realised that Florence's world wasn't just about wallpaper; she was a true artist.

•

With Leonard's departure and the subsequent changes at L. Lewis and Son, Robert moved back to the Sydney suburb of Avalon and took over as company secretary. The new arrangement suited Robert. He saw no future in wallpaper. As Florence remarked in the *Australian Women's Weekly* in 1965, 'My son Robert is running the trucking company now. I once asked him if he liked the wallpaper firm, and he said if it were his he'd put a match to it.' Florence was now free to channel all of her energy into Australian (Hand Printed) Wallpapers Pty Ltd. By the mid-sixties, the business was going global. Florence had established a loyal and influential clientele, exporting to London, New York, Paris, Kuwait, Madrid and Oslo. In fact, business was so brisk, Florence even considered opening an office in Beirut—'the minute they stop fighting', she said (*Sydney Morning Herald*, 1977). Her commissions included designs for Qantas, a chain of hotels in Saudi Arabia and wallpaper for Estee Lauder cosmetics. Her designs decorated the homes of the Benz family in Germany, and the living rooms of Australian socialites including Jill Wran and Lady Sonia McMahon. Her wallpaper even made an appearance on the walls of

Government House in Auckland and the Adelphi Hotel in Perth.

But Florence still wasn't satisfied. Her constant quest for improved designs led to the invention of new and innovative processes in colour, texture and material durability. She experimented in printing with finely ground metals, importing bronze, copper, gold and silver papers from Norway and Sweden when she was unable to find what she wanted in Australia. Metallic colour for use in Australian interior design was unheard of at the time, but before long it was the latest trend. Florence combined these shimmering metallics with fluorescent colours that included lime green, bright yellow, hot pink and sapphire blue.

As kitchens were the focal point for wallpaper at the time, the next step for Florence was to develop washable wallpaper. According to Florence her idea was to create 'a paper from which marks could just be wiped without any use of abrasive or scrubbing' (*Sydney Morning Herald*, 1963). It is possible that Florence got this idea from an early nineteenth century innovation called sanitary wallpapers. These early papers dominated the late-Victorian middle-class market at a time when cleanliness was considered paramount in the home. They were produced from a combination of turpentine and resin and, like Florence's innovation, could also be wiped down. Working closely with an industrial chemist, it took Florence a year to develop a vinyl coat that could be applied without affecting the radiance of her colours. As she said in the *Sydney Morning Herald* in 1963, 'Greens darkened, gold became brittle and red moved out. So I had to find a special formula to meet each of these problems.' Her ingenious vinyl-coat method, which created the opportunity for the hand silkscreen method to be transferred onto other materials such as wood, glass, metal, fabric, blinds and carpets, is still being used around the world today.

On one occassion Florence demonstrated the effectiveness of her method to an unsuspecting *Sydney Morning Herald* journalist who visited her at her Potts Point home in 1963. She picked up 'a sample piece of wallpaper with a lovely matt surface and smeared it with butter. Then [Florence] took a dry tissue and wiped it off—without leaving a mark.' Florence announced, 'At the factory I use axle-grease to demonstrate, but I haven't got any here.'

Florence also made sure that she was up-to-date with interior design trends from overseas. She imported Mylar, a washable man-made product with a mirror surface, from America. Then she matched curtains, pelmets and blinds to her wallpaper, a trend that was popular in Britain. Florence Broadhurst copyists came thick and fast.

Architectural draughtsman David Miles met Florence in 1965 when he was twenty years old. At the time, David was working for high society interior designer Merle du Boulay who, along with a host of other Australian designers, including Leslie Walford, Marion Hall Best, Thomas Harding, Mary White, Malcolm Forbes, Margaret Wardell and Barbara Campbell, signed the document of incorporation for the Society of Interior Designers of Australia in 1964. The vision of these designers was to reinvigorate the organisation, which was established in 1951, to ameliorate and promote the art of interior design. By the late sixties, Florence had become a member of the organisation, along with her contemporaries stylist and author Babette Hayes and Barry Little, of Barry Little Interiors (who was appointed the president at this time).

Merle du Boulay's office was located in Gurner Street, Paddington. David commenced work with Merle in 1963 after he responded to a newspaper advertisement for an employee with drawing skills. It was his lucky break:

I worked for Merle for three years. She was an amazing, high profile designer who had very influential, wealthy clientele. She had a great eye for colour, a great sense of style, she could throw money around and she was well connected socially. In a way, she was another Florence Broadhurst.

While in her employ, David designed murals for private clients that included the American Club on Macquarie Street and the Menzies Hotel on Carrington Street. He also designed tables that had a Corinthian column as the base and a surface encrusted with mosaic tiles. According to David, Merle announced 'out of the blue' that she needed to get some wallpaper done and she sent him to Australian (Hand Printed) Wallpapers in Crows Nest:

> So I drove over in my old beat-up Volkswagen and there was Florence Broadhurst. I had no idea what to expect and she completely and utterly swept me off my feet. She spoke at a million miles an hour and said to me, 'Tell me, what do you do with Merle?' Over the next few months, we developed a rapport and eventually she said to me, 'You should be working for me, not Merle.' She worried me in a way, she seemed so ruthless, so driven. She was someone that I immediately felt that I didn't trust one hundred per cent. I'm not even sure she designed her own wallpapers, I think most of them were rip-offs.

Sally Fitzpatrick agreed that her old boss copied a lot of her designs:

When I worked for her, Flo knocked off everything she could get her hands on. I used to call her the queen of the knock-off. She called it improvising. Most of the time, she didn't design anything if she could get away with it. Her favourite wallpaper designers were Albert Van Luit and William Morris. She simply adored them. We'd go through their sample books and she'd say, 'Fabulous, fabulous, let's do that, darling. I love it'. Then I'd set to work, draw it up and amend it slightly. Of course there was no doubt she did do some originals and she was a very clever artist and designer, but by the time I came on board in 1967, Florence Broadhurst originals were far and few between.

Leslie Walford put it another way:

Florence Broadhurst should be seen as a resource, someone who collected and archived designs; she wasn't really an innovator, just an extremely good business woman who tapped into a niche market. She could produce colours and designs for decorators at breakneck speed. She could produce what you wanted, while you waited.

Barry Little was a little more lenient on his old friend:

Florence did have her detractors, there was no doubt about that. But she was a brilliant woman, whatever she touched turned to gold. When I travelled to America, she would ask me to bring back wallpaper samples for her, which I did. Sure, she used some of the ideas, but she made sure she changed them. Everyone derives their inspiration from somewhere, don't they? What people sometimes forget is that there were other things that Florence did that were totally unique, such as the pearlised effect that she applied to the surface of her prints. I never saw this done anywhere else.

A few months after David Miles met Florence in 1963, he bumped into her at a musical at The Seymour Centre on City Road in Sydney. David recalled that Florence was seated behind he and his wife Cherie during the perform-ance and after it was finished Florence tapped him on the shoulder and invited them back to her Macleay Street apartment for a nightcap.

When we arrived at her apartment there was some-thing that made me feel sorry for her. Here she was in this glamorous apartment, with glamorous clothes, but she was so numb, vague and closed. Deep down I think she was a sad person. She was outlandish, quite nice, but she also seemed like a desperately lonely and pathetic person.

It would take another three years of hard work with Merle du Boulay before David decided to branch out and launch a business of his own in 1966. During the formative stages of his new venture he juggled a variety of jobs that included drawing architectural plans at night, building mosaic tables by day and some design work on the side for Florence. In the late sixties, Florence commissioned David Miles to create a dramatic floor-to-ceiling mural that featured a row of Paddington terrace houses. The design spanned three-and-a-half metres and was printed onto wallpaper panels for The Top of the Cross restaurant in Kings Cross. David and Florence agreed on a price for the commission, but when he showed her the completed mural, she said she wasn't happy. She paid half the agreed fee but still installed it. 'What could I do? She was an extremely difficult person', said David.

In 1969, David and his photographer wife Cherie undertook a road trip around Australia. While he was travelling he couldn't shake his annoyance with the mural deal. He felt that he had been wronged. So, when he returned to Sydney, David Miles decided to set up in opposition to Florence Broadhurst. To learn the ropes, he did a short stint with a silkscreen printing business in

Kogarah; and then David and Cherie developed a range of wallpapers. The name of the company was David Miles Handprints. According to David Miles, Florence's head printer, David Bond, was extremely helpful:

He told me where to buy paper, supplies, paints, you name it. We'd chat and he'd say, 'This is where you get this, this is where you get that'. He probably thought that if I became successful, maybe he could come across and work for me.

It was not long before David Miles Handprints boasted twenty-five designs and thirteen employees.

Toward the end of 1969, the same year that David and Cherie launched their Mortdale-based wallpaper studio, their premises was ransacked. The front door of the fibro factory was broken in, walls were smashed down, windows were shattered, paints were spilt and splashed every-where, screens were broken and splintered and their precious wallpaper had been slashed and destroyed with a sharp blade. When the police arrived and David reported that nothing had been stolen, David alleged they said to him, 'It looks like you've got an enemy.' As David explained:

There is no doubt in our minds that Florence had sent someone in, that she had instigated the crime. Basically we had become more successful than her and she was worried about us becoming a threat. Even when I spoke to David Bond about it, he alluded to the fact that Florence hadn't wanted us to succeed. But what could we do? We couldn't press any charges. All we could do was buy a vicious German Shepherd to protect us and protect the property.

It is hard to establish whether Florence herself was capable of such a heinous act. As Barry Little said, 'I doubt whether Florence was capable of something so despicable. She could be impulsive, but this could have been anyone.'

Either way, it took David Miles and his wife years to recover financially. And despite the hardship they endured, David did finally succeed. His business, which was later renamed David Miles Handprinted Wallcovering, was given a generous helping hand by Arthur G. Wilson of Wilson's Fabric and Wallpapers. David said:

Seventy-five per cent of the business was owned by the Wilson family and twenty-five per cent by us. They set us up in Kent Street in the city, brought us two new cars and sent us on a world trip to look at the world's best design studios, and suddenly Florence was very quiet. There was nothing she could do.

Then in 1976, after an eight-year-long career that included twenty-six design awards and countless front covers on *Vogue Living, Belle* and *Australian House & Garden* magazines, James Hardy Industries bought out Wilson's Fabric and Wallpapers, renamed the David Miles collection as Signature, and David and Cherie branched out on their own to pursue other creative ventures.

It didn't take long for Australian (Hand Printed) Wallpapers to outgrow the leaky shed and annex at Crows Nest. To handle rapid expansion and a dramatic increase in stock (Florence's collection now included Kabuki prints, Spanish scrolls, Florentine and Tudor tapestries, Mexican daises, Birds of Paradise and Ottoman and Imperial brocade), the newly named 'Florence Broadhurst Wallpapers' moved to a spacious new studio-factory in Royalston Street, Paddington. This studio-factory, which in 1970 was valued at one hundred and fifty thousand dollars, was a dramatic improvement on the cramped workshop tucked behind the truck yard. It's gargantuan proportions hailed the beginning of a new era for Florence Broadhurst.

To coincide with the move to her new premises, Florence launched a new advertising campaign in a variety of magazines including *Vogue Living, Australian House &*

Garden and the *Australian Home Journal*. The advertisements claimed that Florence's was 'the only studio of its kind in the world'. It read:

> We print in your choice of colours to any of our 800 designs. Constant exhibition with 12,000 rolls in stock. Featuring the new Mylar Mirror Foil and satin foil papers and patent leather and vinyl look too. We print glass panels, supply furnishing fabrics from Italy and Lamp bases from London. Open Saturdays 10 am–3 pm.

The advertisement also provided contact details for Florence Broadhurst's Melbourne agent, Opat Decorating Services, and highlighted her prestigious international connections: 'Now exporting to America, England, Hawaii, Kuwait, Peru, Norway, Paris, Oslo'. The advertisement also featured a photograph of Florence poised and seated at her desk. She exuded an air of confidence, smug self-satisfaction and looked every inch the sophisticated, savvy business woman of the sixties. She wore a crisp, elegant striped blouse and gold jewellery on her fingers and wrists, and her hair was perfectly teased and set. Her theatrical makeup looked like she has just stepped off the stage. For this (and subsequent) campaigns Florence selected a backdrop of her most eye-catching design: Peacocks—a complex pattern of full-scale birds printed on silver foil paper. Anne-Marie Van de Ven, curator for decorative arts and design at The Powerhouse Museum, which acquired one of these peacock designs in its collection in 2002 after a donor found a rare sample in a bin at her local opportunity shop, describes Peacocks as one of Florence's most mature designs:

> This particular print became Florence's signature design after she posed with it in her business advertisements. In 1976, Jill Wran, wife of newly elected Premier of New South Wales, Neville Wran, decorated the living room of her late Victorian Paddington terrace with Florence's Peacocks paper in shades of blue on silver. For the Premier's wife, and other Sydney socialites, it was considered a bold move at the time to use Florence's papers and that quickly become something of a talking point.

For her new campaign Florence printed the flamboyant peacock pattern on silver foil; the birds were featured in a variety of shades in pink and red. Putting herself in her advertisements was a marketing strategy that harked back to Florence's days as Bobby Broadhurst and Madame Pellier, when she appeared in the *China Press* and *Town and Country News* respectively. But there was something different: the product was now just as flamboyant as the woman.

Florence Broadhurst's new headquarters was a two-storey, one-thousand-square-metre space that could easily accommodate (just as the advertisement claimed) a jumbled library of hundreds of designs and an elegant showroom that featured over six thousand printed samples. There was ample room for a massive workspace, twenty-five staff members and the clients who dropped in daily. There was a staff room and an upstairs office for Florence. It was also a great place for a party.

THE FINAL
YEARS

1970–1977

'I lived in my work and I should have lived above it.'

FLORENCE BROADHURST, THE LONDON DIARIES

The official opening of the Florence Broadhurst Wallpaper studio in Paddington was held on 22 November 1969. Sydney's social set had been anticipating the party for weeks. So had the press. Florence had spent countless hours, days and weeks preparing for the opening of her new headquarters. As well as decorating with potted palms and three-dimensional murals made from tinsel and foil, she had custom-designed reams of wallpaper (that she later gave away at one of her charity events) and issued hand-printed invitations that featured a red swirling print from her collection. Florence also hired a band and a troupe of dancers for entertainment, installed disco balls and laid tables with whole legs of ham, frankfurters, chips and crackers. Wreaths of frangipanis and hibiscus flowers completed the picture.

A newspaper article, aptly titled 'Palm Trees and Psychedelics' recorded the hype generated by the event:

> There is much buzzing and cooing about town at the moment and general forward looking to next Saturday night, which is the very Hawaiian Luau soiree time at Florence Broadhurst's wallpaper making studios in Paddington. It's the most enormous and fascinating place and the high priestess of printed-paper is that flame-haired prima donna of the printing table, the unforgettable Florence. The Black and White Committee of the Royal Blind Society are organising the function. Florence has co-operated to an unbelievable extent, ravaging the Pacific islands for palm trees, printing miles of psychedelic flowery wallpapers and gaying up her vast print rooms for the occasion. She twitters with excitement—as the guests will too on the night to find tables groaning with deliciousness, while Hawaiian music plays and Hawaiian dancers sway (Walford 1969).

To add credibility, glitz and glamour to the event, Florence called on one of her society friends, Lady Hannah Benyon Lloyd-Jones, to officially launch the studio. Lady Hannah was a descendant of the founders of the David Jones department stores in Australia. She was also part of a panel of socialites including newspaper columnist and socialite Nola Dekyvere; ex-international model, television personality and fashion columnist Maggie Tabberer; and high society milliner Jani Lamotte, otherwise known as 'the Countess D'Espinay to people who care for titles' as Daphne Guinness put it so eloquently in the *Bulletin* in 1968. These panelists were to judge a competition for the best-dressed guest at Florence's party. The panel's role was not easy. They had to pick winners for the best hair style, the most glamorous Hawaiian dress and the most exotic Hawaiian shirt from the highly fashionable crowd who had all gone to painstaking lengths to look their best. Guests paraded about the room in kaftans, pant suits, platform shoes and mini-skirts and jostled each other for an opportunity to have their photo taken for the weekend paper.

The party set a precedent that was a tough act to follow but parties at Florence's new headquarters became a regular event on the Sydney social calendar. Most of the gatherings were impromptu, while others—such as her annual Christmas bash—took an age to organise. To keep everything fun, Florence always chose a theme. They ranged from wild sixties psychedelia, to lavish costume parties where invitees were handed a canvas and a paint pot on their arrival and were told to paint each other's portraits. At yet another of Florence's parties guests were invited to bring along photos of themselves as a baby and Florence offered a prize for most identifiable photograph.

Florence always encouraged her guests to dress up and have fun. As one reporter put it in 1971:

The Christmas Spirit abounded in double force at Florence Broadhurst's exciting studios. It was champagne and carols and a late welcome home for Mrs June Golian who sparkled in her silver pants suit. A happy colorful crowd had difficulty keeping up with the fantastic colors of Florence's blinds, foil papers and hand-printed curtain materials. But Mrs Anthony Golian and her husband looked marvellous, 'I'm wearing my Indian bedspread which I've just run up . . .' and with it she tied a brilliant red gypsy scarf around her flowing blonde hair. A great contrast to her husband's white suit worn with a blue shirt and paisley tie. Jocelyn Diethelm was in garden printed voile, and Elsa Jacoby in a giant patterned mu-mu with golden hoze nozzles threaded on orange silk around her neck.

Another article in the *Australian Women's Weekly* in 1971 read: 'Designer Florence Broadhurst's beautifully decorated studio in Paddington was the setting for a cocktail party . . . Guests really dressed up. Even the men, usually happy to let the ladies take fashion honours went colourful and swinging.'

Florence's parties were part of her scheme to infiltrate the society set and thus turn her wallpapers into a high-end commodity. Advertisements for her wallpaper in *Vogue* magazine now read 'Wallpaper for Glamorous Living'.

Just the year before, in June 1968, Sally and her brother Justin Fitzpatrick had chauffeured their beloved Florence to the opening night of the Australian production of 'Hair', which featured the Australian actor Reg Livermore and American singer Marcia Hines. Jim Sharman, the director of the Sydney show, had kindly given Sally tickets for the controversial 'American tribal rock musical', which was written by two New York actors, Gerome Ragni and James Rado. It was being staged in a Kings Cross theatre. As Sally explained:

> Jim Sharman tutored my sister Kate at the National Institute of Dramatic Arts in Sydney and he was a good friend. I had a spare ticket and so I thought the show would be right up Flo's alley, so we decided to make a night of it and have a bit of fun.

In 1968, 'Hair' was a musical that challenged almost every established social norm. It contained drug use, free love and foul language. It opposed the Vietnam War and confronted the issue of inter-racial relations. But it was the infamous nude scene, which lasted between forty seconds and four minutes, depending on who was in the audience, that aroused the most public and press interest. As Jim Sharman explained:

> You had a very puritanical society being confronted with something that was very loud in expressing the need for sexual liberation and I think that if there was a central issue that confronted people it was that one.

It was exactly that sort of response that Harry M. Miller, the entrepreneurial mastermind and producer of the show, was after. He transformed the controversy into publicity.

On the opening night, Sally, Justin and Florence met in a Kings Cross bar. According to Sally:

> There was a real buzz in the air. Everyone who had tickets was dressed up to the nines and was really excited about the event as it had been the focus of so much attention. We started drinking cocktails about two hours before the show was set to kick off, and we bumped into all sorts of people who had tickets, including Leslie Walford who had rocked up in a full-length fur coat. Florence squealed when she saw him;

she simply adored Leslie. We had a few drinks with him and a whole bunch of other people who decided that we looked like we were having fun. It felt like we were drinking cocktails for an eternity. By the time the show was set to start, we were extremely tipsy as we tottered across the road to the theatre.

Even though it did not take long for the threesome to find their seats, Florence missed the entire show. As Sally retold the story:

The moment the curtains went up and the lights went on, Florence passed out and she slept soundly throughout the whole performance. It was absolutely hilarious! Her head lolled back in her seat and she snored extremely loudly. People all around us were looking at Florence and trying to control their fits of laughter. Here we were at this supposedly wild, outrageous musical, yet Florence was the one capturing everyone's attention as she snored her head off. When the show finally finished and the curtain closed, Florence woke with a start and said, 'What? What? Who? Who? Oh . . . fabulous, fabulous, just fabulous, darling.'

●

Florence, who was now in her seventies, could not have been happier in her new environment. The abundance of space was a luxury. She allocated the downstairs space to designing, printing, washing screens and storage, and upstairs to showing off her wares. The lower level of the factory was divided into three separate work areas: a large wallpaper manufacturing space, a central workroom used for drawing, designing and photography, and a space toward the rear for cutting and mixing vinyl. The upper level of the factory featured an eighteen-metre-long show-room, which included a spacious, elegant reception (with an impressive curved counter) concealed with silk-screened glass panels, an office and a staffroom with a washroom, toilet and kitchenette that was accessed via a narrow staircase toward the rear of the building. The showroom was a chaotic tangle of printing screens, rolls of paper, bookshelves, desks and partitions. According to Ben Fitzpatrick, who described the studio-factory as a 'fantastic place to work with an electric atmosphere', Florence seldom came downstairs into the work environment of the building:

> Her zone was upstairs, entertaining the clients. She brought them down from time to time, once or twice a day, just to show off and show them how the wall-paper was produced. Other than that, she was out to one of her charity or social lunches and that was about the only time we ever saw her.

One of the clients who dropped in from time to time was Maggie Tabberer. She recalled:

> I remember having a look through the place and there was literally stuff everywhere. I doubt many people could have worked in all the mess and chaos, but Florence obviously had a method to her madness.

One of these methods was to keep rolls of wallpaper in shelves that lined one end of the upstairs showroom. In front of the shelves was a row of easels that featured Florence's artwork, which by now had progressed to a zany pop-art style. These canvases blocked direct access to the wallpaper, as Sally Fitzpatrick explained:

> It was a strategic move on Flo's part to sell her art. It worked, because not many clients walked out of the studio-factory without one of Flo's paintings under their arm. And as soon as one of her artworks sold, Florence would simply replace it with another one that she had stashed at home. She seemed to have a constant supply.

Another of Florence's methods was to keep a hand-printed record of all the orders she received for her wallpapers.

On 17 November 1972 she wrote in a red notebook, which
is now tattered and worn:

    10 tapestry pearl
    13 galaxy foil
    5 daisy chain
    7 brocade
    5 birds
    1 b/w pomegranates
    1 texture foil
    1 bamboo
    3 yasmin
    9 big tree
    3 roman horses

Florence's showroom was a magnet for visitors and
impromptu staff meetings. It was perpetually filled with
clients, friends and acquaintances who either dropped in
to rifle through sample books, chat about decorating ideas,
catch up on idle gossip or simply indulge in a glass of
sherry or two. Sally reckoned that on most days of the
week, Florence would start drinking at around one or two
in the afternoon:

> Courvoisier was her drink of choice. She'd make a
> cognac cocktail for herself and hand me a gin and

tonic. I'd barely had a drink before I started working there, after all I was only seventeen when I started, but Flo soon taught me how to drink and swear.

On other occasions, Sally recalled that Florence would pop open bottles of champagne, invite her attorney and select staff members up to her office and declare that she had arranged to leave shares in Florence Broadhurst Wallpapers to them. As Sally pointed out with a chuckle:

> Florence used this little party antic as an incentive for her long-term staff to stay on board. She'd give them a glass of sparkling wine and thrust a piece of paper at them that her attorney had drafted and she had signed. I'm sure there are a few people around who still have their piece of paper and are wondering what to do with it!

From the windows of her upstairs office, Florence kept a keen eye on everything that was going on in the workspace below. She surveyed the scene as her employees arrived in the morning and left in the afternoon. She eyed them having lunch and watched her clock at the same time. She observed them mixing colours, printing paper and washing screens. And she watched when they chatted absentmindedly—but not for long. Leslie Walford, who dropped in to the studio-factory frequently, claimed Florence was extremely hard on her workers. As he remembered, she yelled orders at them like a school ma'am. 'Hurry up you fool, stop dawdling. You are so slow this morning,' she'd say. 'Florence had an old fashioned attitude that she was the employer and therefore superior to her workers. She was a strong, determined and fiery character. Certainly, there were people around who were scared stiff of Florence Broadhurst,' he said. Leslie claimed to have been present when one of her painters criticised the quality of her paper, complaining that it was difficult to work with. Her response was characteristically abrupt. 'You incompetent fool, there is nothing wrong with it. Now, get back to work,' she hollered.

Peter Leis agreed his former boss was a tyrant who ruled with an iron fist. He reckoned he was fired for drilling a bolt into the wrong hole. But as Sally explained:

> The trick with Flo was that you just had to work out how to handle her, but many people just didn't understand her at all. She would do things that you or I would never dream of doing. But, she had an amazing sense of humour—we laughed constantly—she was wicked and wonderful.

Sally's brother Ben agreed:

Florence was certainly full on and she could be ruth-
less, there was no doubt about that, but she had a
good heart. She liked to help people. It gave her a
kick. If she didn't respect someone, she gave them a
hard time, it was all a bit of a front as far as I could
see.

Either way, it was a managerial style that with certain
employees didn't earn Florence any popularity points and
it is no surprise that she had a high turnover of staff. On
5 January 1974, one disgruntled employee boldly entered
the factory wearing a stocking over his head. He confronted Florence at her desk in the upstairs showroom
and stole her large black handbag that contained thirteen hundred dollars. When the intruder turned to leave,
Florence tried to grab her handbag. They struggled. He
struck her a number of times, knocked her to the ground
and fractured her left ring finger. Interior designer Barry
Little remembered Florence telling him and his wife,
entertainer Jeannie Little, about the attack:

> She said the attacker came in and tried to get the
> emerald rings off her fingers, but they were unsuc-
> cessful. But Florence said, 'I'm going to get a gun for
> next time they come back.'

On 28 February 1974, Graham Patrick Limbrick was charged with the offence, but this charge was later quashed.

It was an attack that would set most women back on their heels, but it did not ruffle Florence's feathers. Outwardly, she acted as brave, resilient and determined as ever. As Sally Fitzpatrick explained, there was not much that frightened Florence Broadhurst—it was usually the other way around:

> I walked into the studio-factory one day for work and I could hear Florence yelling at the top of her lungs from her office upstairs, 'Fuck you! Get the fuck out of here you fucking bastard! I don't have the time to deal with this. What are you trying to do, send me fucking broke?'

The next thing Sally saw was the accountant who was running for his life down the stairs as Florence stood at the top and pelted him with rolls of wallpaper, account-keeping books, chequebooks and anything she could get her hands on:

> The poor guy, he was really timid and he was having all this abuse and all these objects hurled at him. I was just gobsmacked. But even more baffling was that he kept coming back for more. For three days in a

row he came back to the studio-factory and he got exactly the same response from Florence: 'Fuck you, you fucking bastard!' she'd scream at him. So, he tried another approach and called her, but she just screamed abuse at him and slammed the phone down. I don't know why the accountant wanted to continue working for Florence. It was an amazing scene to watch. Few people knew how completely over-the-top, eccentric and crazy she really was, but I just adored her.

Sally also recalled another similar incident that occurred in 1969, when a water main burst on Royalston Street and some workers turned up to fix it. According to Sally, the workers dug a hole in the road, put a barrier around the hole and set up a mish-mash of equipment directly in front of Florence Broadhurst Wallpapers.

They were based there for about two weeks and Florence was simply and utterly horrified. She thought it would be bad for business and she was not happy with the idea at all. Every morning the workers climbed down a ladder into the hole, spent about fifteen minutes trying to fix the water pipe and then sat around drinking tea for about two hours. This infuriated Florence to the point where she nearly had smoke coming out of her ears. She would work herself up into a frenzy and fling the windows open on the upper level of the studio-factory and yell, 'What are you doing, you fucking bastards? You've been drinking fucking tea for two fucking hours. Get back to fucking work.' Then she threw rolls of wallpapers out the window at them. She'd curse them in the morning, at lunchtime, in the afternoon and then she'd forget about it for a while and quickly dash to the windows again and hurl more abuse and more rolls of wall-paper at them.

Sally added that the workers just sat there, staring wide-eyed at Florence and not uttering a sound. 'They just kept drinking their cups of tea. It was one of the most hilar-ious things I have ever seen,' she said. And on yet another occasion, Sally remembered a young interior decorator who came to see Florence for some advice. According to Sally his breath smelt so disgusting that Florence refused to talk to him until he had gone to the chemist to get something for it:

She actually called the chemist and told them that this poor idiot was coming in and what to give him, and the interior decorator had no choice but to obey her. It was kind of like that with everyone in her life, she was very forceful and persuasive. She had the ability to make people do things that they really didn't want to do, including interior decorators. She would talk them into using paper that at times I was sure they really weren't convinced was quite right. Anyway, the guy went to the chemist and got his medication and then he came back. Florence sat there like nothing had happened and was quite happy to give him whatever advice he wanted.

Florence was still hungry for life and for success. Ethel Mannin's credo rang in her ears: 'Man has not different kinds of energy, but only one energy which he directs into various channels—love, religion, work and money-making.' Florence worked tirelessly and still managed to devote her time (and donate her wallpapers) to a host of charities including the New South Wales Society for Crippled Children, St Margaret's Hospital for Women, Save the Children Fund, the Royal Art Society of New South Wales and the Elizabethan Theatre. Because of all her commitments Florence's beloved painting had now been reduced to a weekend activity. But, being seen at the right events, with the right people, was still a priority.

In 1970 Florence met Her Majesty Queen Elizabeth II, with her daughter Princess Anne, when the British royals briefly visited Australia. And it was around this time that Florence was seen on the arm of a companion who was in his thirties. As Leslie Walford explained, 'She was unstoppable, insatiable. Though she was in her seventies, she had real sex appeal, a twinkle in her eye. She was having an affair with a young, wild party man, which was pretty outrageous because of how old she was. But she still had the X-factor until the day she died.' Janet Mosely agreed that Florence still had what it took, 'She seemed untouchable, aloof—aware of her attractiveness. I'm sure she had a number of sugar daddies or boyfriends. After all, what were all those flowers doing in her bathtub?' Sally Fitzpatrick believed that Florence was never without a young male companion:

In 1973, I was living in Greece and Florence flew over to go on a tour of the islands with me and at the same time try and convince me to come back and work for her. She had a mad scheme up her sleeve that she wanted me to come back and take over the business. When she arrived, it was like a twenty-four-hour whirlwind. She arrived in the morning, I picked her up from the airport, dropped her off at a beautiful hotel right in the heart of the city, she freshened up and then we spent the rest of the day exploring in the searing heat with Flo perched under an outrageous hot pink parasol. You should have seen the looks! Somewhere along the way she'd picked up a young handsome pilot. So, she spent the night having sex with him at the hotel and the next day we checked out the islands and she flew back to Australia.

On another occasion Sally recalled walking up the stairs of the studio-factory, only to discover her boss and a young man in an uncompromising position on Florence's desk. 'As I walked up the stairs I heard the guy say, "I think someone's coming," to which Flo replied, "Oh, it's only Sally, don't worry". Then she roared with laughter.'

After years of hard work in the wallpaper business, Florence now had the time, and the money, to do what she loved best: travel. Some of her jaunts were for pleasure, some were for business and she frequently combined the two. In 1972 and 1973 she took extended trips to Singapore, London, New York and Zurich. By day she promoted her wallpapers, by night she stayed at lavish hotels that included the well-appointed St Moritz Hotel on Central Park in New York and the exclusive Raffles Hotel in Singapore. It was at the latter hotel that she had the good fortune of landing a commission to design wallpaper for the luxurious interiors. According to Leslie Walford, 'When Florence got the job at Raffles, all the interior designers in Sydney were green with envy.'

Florence had also conquered the United States. As one reporter commented: 'Florence Broadhurst, well-known artist and wallpaper designer, has returned from a world trip . . . She was delighted with the success of her wallpapers, particularly in the United States, where she was well received and has now established a firm market'. Her well-heeled clientele in the United States provided a profitable network for Florence that started through an interior decorator named Bob Thayer. Florence had originally met Bob in 1964 while he was working as the American consul in Australia. When Bob retired in the mid-sixties he moved to Arlington, Virginia, where he and his wife went into the interior decorating business. As Florence explained to the *Sun* in 1965: 'They took samples of my work with them and this has created a demand I can't meet.'

For her new American market, Florence harked back to the paintings she produced while motoring around the outback. She created 'designs mostly based on Australiana—stylised boomerangs, the wallaby hunt, and native wildflowers'. To ensure her market was cornered, Florence applied the marketing techniques that she had perfected in Shanghai, London and Sydney. Florence knew her clients couldn't come to meet her, so she went to meet them. Throughout the seventies New York and Hawaii became pit stops on her relentless lecture tours that she gave to women in the United States. Florence appeared on television and radio voicing her opinions on business, success and world affairs. When she returned she said:

> I was absolutely astonished by the response to my papers. People were astounded that work of this calibre could be done in the southern hemisphere. I had tapped into a highly lucrative overseas market.

It was not long before the Florence Broadhurst Wallpaper network was global and she celebrated her success. On 30 May 1973, the *Wentworth Courier* noted: 'Before she leaves for Bahrain to do a bit of décor for the Middle East Hotel Chain, Florence Broadhurst threw one of those huge parties of hers at her Paddington studio on Friday. As well as her trip to the Middle East, Florence will also visit Qantas offices around the world to give them a new look including some murals of Australian bark.'

Now when Florence travelled she carried with her a certificate of introduction from the State premier's office. It was a certificate that helped pave the way for many hassle-free journeys.

> The Bearer of this Credential, Miss Florence Broadhurst, as a respected resident of this State, is proceeding on a visit to: Great Britain, the Continent of Europe and the United States of America. Any courtesy that may

be afforded to her will be valued on her part and will be appreciated by this Government. Signed Premier of the State of New South Wales in the Commonwealth of Australia.

Other courteous letters of introduction that Florence sourced from a host of social connections could be found in the depths of her handbag. An associate from Victor Dekyvere & Company, a retailer on Kent Street in Sydney, wrote one of them: 'A very good friend of mine, Miss Florence Broadhurst, will be visiting Hong Kong on the 3rd July. She has never been in Hong Kong before and she would like some advice as to where to buy cameras, pearls, etc.'

New horizons meant other things to Florence besides travel. In her spare time, Florence had taken up gambling. It was an addiction that started innocently. On the odd occasion she purchased a lottery ticket when she picked up a copy of the *Sydney Morning Herald* at the newsagency. She was also seen frittering money away on a regular basis at the City Tatts on Pitt Street. But when she became friendly with a select crew who frequented the Royal Randwick Racecourse her new passion evolved into something far more serious—horseracing. It gave Florence a thrill to watch the handsome three-year-old thoroughbreds test their stamina on the mile-and-a-half (two-and-a-half-kilometre) long track. It was a sport that combined all the ingredients that got her blood pumping: taking a chance, the prospect of winning, frocking up and free-flowing champagne. It was the sport of kings. But Florence was never cut out to be an observer. Sipping chardonnay and punting trackside soon lost their appeal. So, with a friend, Mrs E. Davis, she devised a scheme to purchase Petals, a two-year-old filly. Though the legacy of Petals might not be etched into the Australian annals, she was a good investment and turned out to be a moderate success, winning a number of races. And now, at her parties, Florence could say, 'I own a racehorse.'

Florence also set her sights on finding a new home that reflected the glitz and glamour of her lifestyle. At some point in the late sixties, Florence got rid of her Macleay Street apartment and shifted into a glamorous new pad. The address was Unit 13, Belgravia Gardens, 60 Darling Point Road, Darling Point. According to Leenne Rose, whose mother Sherdene purchased the property in 1978, a year after Florence had died, 'The apartment was really garish, over-the-top and in your face. We had Christmas there every year for years, but we never had to decorate a single thing. Unit number thirteen just looked like Christmas all the time.' When Sherdene bought the three-bedroom apartment it was fully furnished, and she kept it in its original state until she died in 1996. The home had outstanding views of Sydney from almost every room—to the south there was the Sydney Harbour Bridge and the city lights, while to the north there were views of the neighbouring suburb of Double Bay and the distant hill that rises up beyond Watson's Bay to Vaucluse. The apartment had wallpaper on every wall—even a dramatic metallic and white design in the cramped bathroom and toilet that also featured mirrors on every wall. Leenne described it as, 'Like a make-up room in a theatre—you could see yourself from every possible angle, even the back of your head'. The entrance and hallway were pasted over with the same design that appeared in the bathroom, while the living and dining rooms were embellished with a marblised, repetitive print finished with a smart gold fleck. The bedroom was covered in dramatic, large silver and hot pink tulips. But the pièce de résistance was also in the bedroom—a theatrical queen-sized four-poster bed with a Thai silk canopy in hot pink, curtains (also in hot pink) laced up to each bed post and a quilted, padded bed head that was elegantly scalloped at the edges. It was the colour of a glass of pinot noir. 'I don't know how mum slept in the damn thing for all those years, but somehow she did,' said Leenne, who donated remnants of the bed to the Powerhouse Museum in Sydney.

Leenne also claimed there were four artworks in the living room. Two of these (an undulating landscape and sizeable female nude that 'nearly took up the whole wall') were painted and signed by Florence; a third was a moody sketch of a woman with 'soft, doe-like eyes'; the fourth was a portrait of Florence in a long, flowing chartreuse dress, with her legs crossed and one bejewelled hand holding the other in her lap. The only other feature in the painting appears in the upper right hand corner. It is a skeletal, ghost-like figure that floats in profile in the air and faces Florence. According to Leenne, who still owns the portrait, the artist was the Canadian wife of Georgios Kostantis, the Greek Consulate in Australia in 1977. Leenne claimed that the portrait was painted three weeks before Florence died. She said that when her mother Sherdene asked the Greek Consular's wife why she had included the figure in the portrait, she could not explain her motive. Leenne thought the inclusion of the figure was eerie. 'It looks like death coming toward her,' she said. While it is doubtless the figure is a chilling addition to the painting, it is hard to ascertain whether the image was an original part of the painting or whether it was inserted by an unknown artist at a later date.

•

In 1971, when Florence was seventy-two-years-old she won a part in a little known Australian short film called *David and Pyewacket*. Two years later, the film won the coveted Milli Award for the Australian Cinematographer of the Year. Other films that won this award include *Storm Boy*, *My Brilliant Career*, *Gallipoli* and, later, *Babe*. Directed by feature film veteran Donald Wynne the film was written by his wife, Diana, and set in New South Wales in the 1880s. It is seen through the eyes of a child. Florence's cameo role is as an old woman. A reporter from the *Sun-Herald* commented on her appearance, 'Doing needlepoint, seated in front of the good old Georgian silver piled on an afternoon tea tray was—guess who?—Florence Broad-hurst, as a rather wicked old lady' (Walford, 1971).

Released during the Christmas period at Brisbane's Forum Cinema, *David and Pyewacket* appeared as a support to the Ken Russell film *The Boyfriend*. One reviewer described it as a 'film made of gold'. Another reviewer was effusive about an event at the New Art Cinema in Sydney where the film was a feature:

Once the evening was in full swing (we) called everyone to the auditorium and encouraged Florence Broadhurst and nine-year-old David Wynne to mount the stage and throw streamers at the audience before we enjoyed two short movies, one of which was "David and Pyewacket" written by the young star's mother, Diana Wynne, and directed by Donald Wynne, his father. After this delightful film depicting a dreamy childhood world in the New South Wales countryside of 90 years ago, we delved into a lavish supper, then danced like mad to the music of the moment by the Sounds Mobile Discotheque (Walford, 1971).

Florence looked like a million dollars on the night. She danced until dawn and worked until dusk, when the party started all over again. She appeared as vigorous and healthy as ever. But her health was failing. In 1972, Doctor Henley Harrison, a Macquarie Street specialist, diagnosed Florence with sensory-neural deafness and issued her with hearing aids. Florence concealed her new accessories with strategically styled hair and gaudy gold earrings. Most people were fooled and not many knew she wore them. But, being hard of hearing was only one of Florence's concerns. She was almost blind from cataracts creeping over her eyes.

When a friend told Florence about the Peter Stephan Cell Therapy Clinic in London, which claimed to offer an elixir of youth, she was sold. Without blinking an eye she contacted the homeopath in 1973, a year after she started wearing hearing aids. Dr Stephan's claim was that he could stimulate the regeneration of underdeveloped, diseased and age-damaged organs. He made controversial claims that his brand of therapy improved the tone, texture and elasticity of skin, stabilised weight, firmed sagging breasts and treated sexual dysfunction. According to Dr Stephan his ultimate aim was 'to give more years to life' and to 'make all the organs struck by old age capable once more of functioning properly'.

Dr Stephan injected new cell material taken from the foetuses, embryos and organs of young and unborn animals into his patients' organs. Injecting lamb placenta into his patients, he said, would replace dying cells. Dr Stephan's theories were later dismissed by the General Medical Council as 'a load of old rhubarb' (Strassmann, 1994). But Florence booked and paid for an intensive two-week course of cell therapy at a cost of two hundred and fifty pounds, and on 12 July 1974 she met Dr Stephan in London. She stayed at a nearby hotel, undertook her course and returned to Australia feeling like a new woman.

This was not the first or the last time that she had work done to her body and face. David Miles remembered visiting Florence in hospital in the sixties when she was recovering from cosmetic surgery:

My wife and I heard she was in hospital to get something done to her neck. We felt sorry for her, so we went and paid her a visit but we had no idea she was getting cosmetic surgery done. We hadn't really heard of anyone getting it done before, not back then anyway. It was considered taboo. But later, when she had recovered, my employer at the time, Merle du Boulay said, 'Didn't you know Florence gets facelifts all the time? I thought everyone knew.' When I next saw Florence, there was no doubt she looked different, kind of like a scrawny chook with her skin pulled tight.

Judy Korner, her beautician for twenty years offered this explanation:

Cosmetic surgery was a new concept in the sixties and seventies. There were only a handful of women getting it done in Sydney at the time, I think Florence was one of them. It was a big decision back then because the process was much cruder than it is today. But Florence looked fantastic, it was all part of her image to look eternally youthful, successful and glamorous. She was like a grand dame from the English theatre.

Sally Fitzpatrick recalled Florence telling her she'd had three facelifts (other reports suggest that she had five):

On one of these occasions she and a girlfriend had one done together and then as a reward they went on a holiday on a cruise ship. But while they were out at sea, her girlfriend's face dropped and she was forced to come home to Sydney. She left Florence to recover in peace.

In the mid-seventies, Florence also had some surgery done to remove the cataracts from her eyes, but as Sally Fitzpatrick explained the 'surgeon' that Florence chose was questionable:

Florence sent me a number of postcards from the Philippines, where she had gone to see a witch doctor who apparently didn't use anything but his hands to cure his patients—no drugs, no scalpels or anything. I've seen documentaries on these doctors who just reach inside people and pull out the offending organ or whatever. But it is all just a scam. It's voodoo. Florence wrote to me and said, 'Darling, guess what? I've just had surgery at the witch doctors. It's a miracle, I can see.'

But it seems that Florence had talked herself into it. When Sally asked her a few years later how her vision was Florence replied despondently, 'It's much better, but not as good as what it was.' As Sally explained, it upset Florence that she could not see as well as she was once able to. 'She was a very visual person and it definitely got her down, like her body was betraying her.'

Regardless, in the winter of her life Florence still looked and felt great. Her figure was svelte, she wore stylish clothes and her cosmetic therapy meant that it was impossible to tell her real age. When she was asked how old she was, she said she was forty-eight and most people believed her.

•

At 6 am on 16 October 1977 John Griffith Chamberlain, who had lived next door to Florence's Paddington studio-factory since the late sixties, peered out his window. He noticed that the front door of the Florence Broadhurst Wallpaper studio was open and that the lights had been left on. John, a widower in his seventies, drove up the hill to the Paddington Police Station, where he spoke to Sergeant Patrick Leembrugen, the officer on duty. The sergeant and his colleague, Constable Russell, drove directly to the factory. They arrived at 10.45 am and noticed nothing unusual on the lower level, so they walked up the narrow staircase to the first floor. Leembrugen noted that a large black handbag was open on the elegant curved desk in the reception, and two beige wallets (that had apparently been taken from the bag) lay on the desk. Beyond the reception, there were two doors, one that led into the main showroom and another that led into the kitchenette. Constable Russell went into the main showroom, while his colleague Leembrugen entered the kitchenette. Leembrugen walked through the kitchen and, before he opened the door to the washroom, which contained a hand basin, a mirror, a chest of drawers, shelves and a paper towel dispenser, he noticed a hearing aid and tea towel on the floor. He pushed the washroom door ajar and noticed that the carpet in the washroom was sodden and there was a red bag on the floor. He then pushed the toilet door open. He was shocked to discover a lifeless Florence wedged between a blood-spattered wall and the toilet.

The two police officers immediately left the building and radioed for assistance from their car. A short time later, detectives from the homicide squad, which included Detective Sergeant Greer, Detectives Hollis and Hansen, and a government medical officer, Doctor Oettle, arrived at the studio factory.

At 11.50 am Detective Senior Constable Kerry Riddell from the scientific investigation section arrived to examine Florence's body, take photographs of the premises and collect evidence. He noted that a small wall safe in the upstairs office (that was normally concealed by one of Florence's portraits) had been exposed. The portrait was on the floor leaning against a wall. He also noted that the doors of the adjacent steel lockers had been left ajar. At 12.15 am, Senior Constable Schell arrived to conduct a thorough search for fingerprints on the lower and upper levels of the factory. And later that afternoon, the Government Contractor removed Florence's body and took it to the city morgue, where the following day her body was identified by her ex-husband, Leonard, who gave his address as Perth, Western Australia, and her son Robert, who gave an address in a suburb of Sydney.

•

Theories about Florence's murder abound, most of them unsubstantiated. Robbery appears to have been a strong motive, but when it was learned in 1992 that one of her employees was married to the half-brother of 'granny killer' John Glover, by then behind bars, police had another avenue of enquiry. Mike Hagan, a detective inspector involved in the investigation of the murders of six elderly women and the attempted murder of another on Sydney's North Shore between March 1989 and March 1990, said that while Glover admitted to those crimes, he never admitted to killing Florence. 'There are however, similarities,' noted Hagan, who is now retired from the New South Wales police force.

Interior designer Barry Little he said recalled Florence telling him that she was involved in a financial deal and 'they'd taken her money and so she was going to spill the beans'. Peter Leis and John Lang supported this theory.

As John Lang said, 'She couldn't help herself, she couldn't keep her mouth closed and they [her murderer] wanted to shut her up.' Robert Lloyd Lewis thought this was unlikely. 'She discussed every financial transaction with me and nothing like this was ever discussed. I have no knowledge of the financial thing referred to.'

According to Sally Fitzpatrick, it was doubtless that Florence had her enemies:

I remember one weekend she went on a harbour cruise that had been organised for a group of A-listers. One of the guests was a man who was a highly prominent and well-respected public figure. He was married and had children, but unbeknownst to his wife, he had turned up on the boat with his lover—another man. During the cruise the two men were all over each other, it was quite obvious they were together. Florence was horrified by his lack of scruples—that he was lying to his wife and lying to society. So, she spent the rest of the week on the phone calling every single society person she knew to 'out' this guy. Florence probably ruined his career and his life.

All the customers that were present on the day that Florence died—including the man in the green shirt, his female companion, the middle-aged Jewish couple and

Sue McCarthy—were interviewed and fingerprinted, as were Florence's staff, her neighbours and members of her family. As Sally Fitzpatrick recalled, 'A lot of people were questioned and some staff members had the entire contents of their homes emptied into the back yard. For a few months life for these people was hell.'

•

Florence Broadhurst's murder has never been solved, with other rumoured suspects including a young lover (who was also questioned by police before being released), an ex-employee and a business associate. The police file remains open.

In the aftermath of her death, police offered a $10 000 reward for information on her killer and they still want to know about the whereabouts of two valuable rings that had been stolen from her. The rings were described in the police report as:

One single-cut diamond ring, cape white coloured stone of 3.4 carats. Brilliant cut, with two baguette diamonds on shoulder. Ring has platinum shank. One ladies dress ring, single emerald, emerald cut, high quality stone, rich in colour with minimal inclusion. Approximately two carats. Emerald surrounded by ten pure white diamonds approximately 10–15 points each.

Both emeralds and diamonds all in the one raised
setting. Ring has a platinum shank.

In 1977, these rings were valued at more than $50 000.
Leonard claimed in the *Australian Women's Weekly* in 1977
that just a month before his ex-wife's death he had warned
her about 'working in the factory alone' and told her 'to
be careful about wearing her jewellery'. He then went on
to say, 'I'm grief stricken they have cost her life.' But we
might never know with certainty whether the motivation
for her gruesome murder was a robbery or whether it
was simply made to look that way.

•

A funeral for Florence was held at St Mark's Anglican
Church at Darling Point. The elegant gothic revival building
was packed with shocked and devastated mourners. Plain-
clothes detectives mingled with the congregation as they
searched for clues that might lead to her killer. The rector,
Reverend J. Whild, gave a touching and pertinent service.
When he finished, Leonard took his place at the pulpit
and read an abbreviated version of the manifesto that
Florence had written when she was a fifteen-year-old
Mount Perry schoolgirl. His words echoed the sum of
parts of her life cut short by tragedy:

When Florence turned her back on her Queensland upbringing, it was to forge her own path and live out her own destiny, no matter what the consequences—'*I will be selfish, for ultimately I will gratify and bring happiness to myself*'. When the revolution in China resulted in the premature closure of her performing arts academy, Florence abandoned Shanghai without regret and made bigger plans to conquer Europe—'*I will fail and in failing I will try again. I will fall and in falling, climb*'. When the early days of her English life came to a bitter end after her divorce from Percy Kann and the closure of the Pellier dress salon, Florence forged ahead and did not '*blame others for (her) many sorrows and defeats, for man has but himself to blame for failure*'. When her second husband had an affair with, and married, his young lover, Florence did not wallow in her misery but once again, she drew on her inner strength and personal resources by launching a new life and career for herself. Australian (Hand Printed) Wallpaper, and later Florence Broadhurst Wallpapers, was the crowning success in a creative and fearless life lived with conviction, focus and self-belief. Despite the unexpected twists and turns of life, Florence always survived—'*I will grasp the goodness and the beauty of life, and throw away the ugliness and bitterness. I will turn my face to the light; yet remember the darkness that lies behind and around me*'.

Florence might have been called many things in her lifetime—such as an overbearing tyrant or a vain eccentric—but she carried with her a strong sense of righteousness and a wonder at the miracle of creation— *'I will thank Him for the glorious beauty of the world at sunset, for the unbearable sweetness of song. For the million, million things which lie in wait for us every hour of the day, to please our sight and fill our eyes with perfection.'*

It was not exactly the kind of funeral that Florence had envisaged for herself. Sally Fitzpatrick claimed that when Florence came to see her in Greece in 1973, her old friend mused:

> She'd had a good life, so she wanted something like an Irish wake for her funeral. She said she wanted three days of madness, with everybody drinking Courvoisier and toasting her. I suggested that everyone could turn up wearing a red wig with false red eyelashes and plexi-glass rings on every finger. Florence loved that idea and we had a good laugh about it over a few cocktails in a bar in Athens.

On 20 October 1977, five days after her death, Florence was cremated at the Northern Suburbs Crematorium in the Sydney suburb of North Ryde. Her memorial, marked '128 MG6', is basic, unadorned and seemingly forgotten even though her plaque reads: 'In Loving Memory of Florence Maud Broadhurst 28.7.1899—15.10.1977. Always Remembered'. Her ashes lie deep in the heart of an elegantly manicured memorial garden on the edge of Lane Cove National Park.

In the shadows of ghost-like pine trees, clipped conifers and Morton Bay figs with their tangled understudy of twisted roots Florence's plaque joins other famous names whose final resting place is at the crematorium, including May Gibbs, Banjo Patterson, Sir Joseph Cook, Sir William McMahon and Michael Hutchence, who lies two feet away from her. The remains of these celebrated Australians are scattered throughout the immaculately landscaped site. And as is always the case at cemeteries or crematoriums, there is a feeling of serenity and the presence of death that dances on your skin. But there is also a feeling of peace.

Florence being Florence, she would want to have the last word. And just like her friend Sally said, she would not want us to mourn the loss of her life, rather she would want us to rejoice in the joy of her life itself. As Florence herself said:

Do not leave your flowers upon the graves that be in cemeteries, but rather keep your money, your time, your moods of generous emotion for handing out bouquets for the living.

Epilogue

*P*eople's legacies are strange. A lifetime is a long time—with countless phases, changes and up-heavals, but in the end a person is remembered (if they are remembered at all) for a mere handful of things. Though we know that the sum of Florence Broadhurst's life was much more than her wallpaper designs or her unfortunate murder—these are the things for which she is remembered.

Since I penned the articles about Florence in 1999, contemporary designers have had their own love affair with Florence Broadhurst. Fashion designer Akira Isogawa was the first to spot the potential of her collection. In 2000 and 2002 Akira featured a jacket, skirt and dress printed with Florence's designs in his Paris shows. According to Akira:

When I worked with her prints, I didn't feel like I was making such a great leap away from what I was already doing and designing. In a strange way, I felt like Florence and I were totally in synch.

The following year (and every season since) Zimmerman have used her prints (blossoms, hibiscus flowers, lilies and the like) in their swimwear and clothing collections. And New Zealand-based designer Karen Walker incorporated Florence's work into her 2001 and 2003 collections that included the quirky 'Pups' and 'Horses' prints. As Karen explained:

For Pups we designed hoodies, t-shirts, singlets, jewellery, mini-skirts, buttons and bags. And for Horses we also did shirts, dresses, t-shirts, singlets, while the wallpaper featured in our stores. They're very beautiful—all of them. Florence was a great designer. I love how her work is emotive and figurative. The two that I chose were quite grand in an art deco kind of way.

The press (*i-D*, US *Vogue* and *In Style* UK magazines among them) responded just as effusively Karen.

Australian interior designers were the next in line to catch the Broadhurst bug. Funkis, a Sydney-based homewares store, launched a range that included lampshades, cushion covers, fabric screens, upholstery fabric and bags based on Florence's designs. Next, Customweave Carpets and Rugs gave her work a new twist when they launched a collection of rugs embossed with her bamboo, butterfly and Japanese-inspired floral work. Then Melbourne-based designer Matthew Butler of Bluesquare came up with the novel concept of covering his angular Polar chairs with filmy lengths of her fabric. As Matthew said:

> The idea with the chairs was to fuse fashion and furniture. I'd seen Akira Isogawa use Florence's designs with his dresses and I loved it. But I wanted to take the idea one step further and cover something more solid and lasting with her designs. I love her graphics and the strength of her designs.

So Florence Broadhurst's name is again on everyone's lips and her designs appear everywhere: on the walls of exclusive nightclubs, bars and cafes such as Will and Toby's in Darlinghurst, Omega on King Street, the Lotus Bar in Potts Point, the Tank nightclub in Sydney's cental business district and the exclusive club Soho House in New York. They are splashed across the walls of sleek retail outlets such as Oroton, Leona Edmiston, Allanah Hill and Mimco, and in homes designed by interior designers such as Greg Natale and Tina de Salis. Florence's designs are available across the globe in Sydney, Wales, Scotland and the United States and in England at the exclusive Self-ridge's store.

The Florence Broadhurst revival was also recorded in the press. In 2000, *Wallpaper** magazine featured a six-page spread of her designs. In October 2002, *Casa Vogue* in Italy published an article called 'Silvering the Wall', a triple double-page tribute to Florence Broadhurst. It was printed on silver foil with black and purple inks. The following year (August 19, 2003) the *International Herald Tribune* in Paris also paid tribute to Florence in their article, 'From the outback, a pioneer of design'. This prompted New York-based fashion designer Diane von Furstenburg to contact Sydney's Powerhouse Museum to enquire after Florence and her work. Then, in February 2003 (not long after the Florence Broadhurst Collection took out a pres-tigious Gold Award at the 2002 Decorex Design show in London), Florence's Peacocks design, the one I had so adoringly looked up to as a child, was featured on the cover of *indesign*, an Australian interior, architecture and product magazine.

But more importantly than the revival of Florence's work, is finding the person responsible for her death. In June 2004, the New South Wales Police launched the Unsolved Homicide Unit, a team of detectives who will investigate 400 unsolved murder cases committed between 1970 and the year 2000—Florence Broadhurst's case is among these. As Detective Superintendent Paul Jones said:

> For years now, while murder has been investigated by police, there has not been a consistent method for the review of old cases. For the families involved in these cases there has been no closure. This new homicide unit offers the opportunity for these families to have their cases reviewed and examined through fresh eyes. It is our wish that with this system of review, combined with the advances in technology, the NSW Police can exhaust every possibility in each individual murder case.

More than wallpaper stuck to walls and dresses on catwalks it is my sincere hope that the new unit of nine investigators will uncover a few more mysteries in the life of Florence Broadhurst . . .

Acknowledgements

Thank you to Gregory, my husband, for putting up with my Broadhurst obsession and for being so wonderfully supportive; Fitzroy Boulting, my literary agent, for your impeccable housekeeping; Jo Paul, my publisher at Allen & Unwin, for putting up with all the twists and turns of the journey; Colette Vella for your scrupulous editing; and Joanne Holliman, Jeanmarie Morosin and all the other staff members at Allen & Unwin who have worked with me on this book.

Also thanks to Anne Marie Van de Ven for your invaluable suggestions, time and the foreword; Dad for chauffeuring Evie and me half way around Queensland; Pat 'I told you I was sick' Smith and Jim 'the quiet one' Smith for the fish cakes and the grand tour of Mount Perry; and Marlene Wilson, Anne O'Loughlin and Bonnie Stacey for the history on the Broadhurst family. As well, thanks to Ted Bettiens; Anne McGoverne; Kate, Sally and Ben Fitzpatrick; David and Cherie Miles; Barry and Jeannie Little; Maggie and Brooke Tabberer; Akira Isogawa (and Penny, his assistant); Karen Walker; Leona Edmiston; Nicky and Simone Zimmerman; Matthew Butler from Bluesquare; Carina Enstrom Gibb from Funkis; Neil Power from Customweave; Bryan Fitzgerald and Casey Khik from Chee Soon & Fitzgerald; Robert Garrick, Greg Natale, Paul Jones, Mike Hagan from the NSW Police Force; John Lang; Peter Leis; Leenne Rose; Leslie Walford; Janet Moseley; Annie Georgeson and Judy Korner.

Bibliography

Note: Many of the quotes in this book came from magazine and newspaper clippings in the Broadhurst personal papers held at the New South Wales State Library. As the articles did not always have full publication details that information was not available when compiling this bibliography.

Australia Magazine, 18 May 1954, 'Ambassadress with a Paintbrush', Broadhurst, personal papers, New South Wales State Library MLMSS41 45

Australian Cinematographers Society, A Brief History, 2001, www.acs.asn.au

Australian Women's Weekly, 25 August 1965, 'Export Success Stories', Broadhurst, personal papers, New South Wales State Library MLMSS41 45

Australian Women's Weekly, 1971, Broadhurst, personal papers, New South Wales State Library MLMSS41 45

Australian Women's Weekly, 16 November 1977, 'A Man Remembers the Woman He Loved', pp 28–29

Australian, 16 October 1968, 'Artist Wants to Cure People of Timid Syndrome', Broadhurst, personal papers, New South Wales State Library MLMSS41 45

Australian, Broadhurst, personal papers, New South Wales State Library MLMSS41 45

Barker, A.W., 1992, *What Happened When: A Chronology of Australia 1788–1990*, 2nd edition, Allen & Unwin, Sydney

Bennett, K., 1990, *Kit Bennett's Memories of Mount Perry: The Land and People*, Kit Bennett, Queensland

Bilgora, A., 2003, *Dame Clara Butt (1872–1936)*, www.wyastone.co.uk/nrl/pvoce/7912c.html

Broadhurst, F., 'The Impact of Dunkirk', *Daily Mirror*, 10 July 1958, p 30

Broadhurst, personal papers, New South Wales State Library MLMSS41 45

Bundaberg Daily News and Mail, 31 July 1927, 'Five Years Abroad Experiences in the East'

Clifford, N.R., 1990, 'Society and Culture' in *Spoilt Children of Empire: West-erners in Shanghai and the Chinese Revolution of the 1920s*, University Press of New England, pp 60–78

Curby, P., 2001, 'South Pacific Playground' in *Seven Miles from Sydney*, Manly Council, Sydney, pp 251–270

Daily Telegraph, 1954, 'Artist to Paint the Story of Australia', Broadhurst, personal papers, New South Wales State Library MLMSS41 45

Daily Telegraph, 25 February 1958, 'Queen Mother Renewed Old Acquaintance', p 32

Daily Telegraph, 1990, 'Obituaries, Patience Strong', www.originofnations.org/books,%20papers/patience_strong.pdf

'Elizabeth, wife of George VI and Queen Mother', 2004, National Archives of Australia, www.naa.gov.au/Publications/research_guides/guides/royalty /pages/chapter10.htm

Field, A., 1999, 'Selling Souls in Sin City: Shanghai Singing and Dancing Host-esses in Print, Film and Politics, 1920–1949' in *Cinema and Urban Culture in Shanghai, 1922–1943*, Zhang, Y. (ed.), Stanford University Press, Cali-fornia, pp 99–103

Giffney, P., 'Personality Parade', Broadhurst, personal papers, New South Wales State Library MLMSS41 45

Guinness, D., 1968, 'Out and About, Bulletin', The Black and White Tradition, www.firstunion.com.au/black&white/bwtradition.htm

Hanchao, L., 1999, 'Escaping the Shantytown' in *Beyond the Neon Lights: Everyday Shanghai in the Early Twentieth Century*, University of Cali-fornia Press, Berkeley

Hanchao, L., 1999, 'In Search of an Urban Identity' in *Beyond the Neon Lights: Everyday Shanghai in the Early Twentieth Century*, University of Cali-fornia Press, Berkeley

Hillier, R., 1970, *A Place Called Paddington*, Ure Smith, Sydney

Jobson, S., *Women's Day*, 12 October 1964, 'Spotlight on Gay Ball Decor'

Kobe Herald, 2 April 1924, Broadhurst, personal papers, New South Wales State Library MLMSS41 45

Lambert, T., 2003, 'A Short History of London', www.localhistories.org /london.html

Loftie, W.J., 1885, *Orient Line Guide: Chapters for Travellers by Sea and by Land*, Marston, Searle & Rivington, London

McCart, N., 2002, 'Technical Data and Description', www.the-orvieto.co.uk /index.php?page=rmsorvieto5

MacCarthy, F., 1982, *British Design Since 1880: A Visual History*, 1st edition, Humphries, London

Manchuria Daily News, 28 March 1924, Broadhurst, personal papers, New South Wales State Library MLMSS41 45

Mannin, E., 1938, *Daily Express*, Broadhurst, personal papers, New South Wales State Library MLMSS41 45

'Marriage of HRH The Princess Elizabeth and Lieutenant Philip Mountbatten on 20 November 1947 in Westminster Abbey', www.newsrelease-archive.net/coi/dept/GQB/coi4545d.ok

Penang Gazette and Straits Chronicle, Broadhurst, personal papers, New South Wales State Library MLMSS41 45

People Magazine, 16 January, 1963, Broadhurst, personal papers, New South Wales State Library MLMSS41 45

People, 16 January 1963, 'Silent Wallpaper', Broadhurst, personal papers, New South Wales State Library MLMSS41 45

'She Came to Rest and Stayed to Paint', Broadhurst, personal papers, New South Wales State Library MLMSS41 45

'Exhibition of Paintings, Florence Broadhurst's Art', Broadhurst, personal papers, New South Wales State Library MLMSS41 45

'She Pioneers in the Desert for Her Art', Broadhurst, personal papers, New South Wales State Library MLMSS41 45

Reade, E., 1975, *The Australian Screen: A pictorial history of Australian Film Making*, Lansdowne Press, Melbourne

Rogers, P., 1968, 'The Paper Makers', *Australian Home Journal*

Royle, M., 1998, *Perry's Past: A Centenary History of the Perry Shire*, The Perry Shire Council, Queensland

Starr, A. and Morice, J. 2000, *Paddington Stories*, Andrew Starr & Associates, Sydney

Sun, 7 February 1962, 'Shares New Field of Art', Broadhurst, personal papers, New South Wales State Library MLMSS41 45

Sun, 29 September 1965, Broadhurst, personal papers, New South Wales State Library MLMSS41 45

Sunday Australian, 28 November 1971, 'Jingle Bells and Champagne', Broadhurst, personal papers, New South Wales State Library MLMSS41 45

Sunday Mirror, 28 June 1964, Broadhurst, personal papers, New South Wales State Library MLMSS41 45

Sutherland, D., 1999, 'The Admission of Women to the House of Lords', www.qub.ac.uk/cawp/research/pitor.htm

Sydney Morning Herald, 18 April 1963, 'Wallpaper that Wipes Clean', Broadhurst personal papers, New South Wales State Library MLMSS41 45

Sydney Morning Herald, 20 May 1966, Broadhurst, personal papers, New South Wales State Library MLMSS41 45

Thompson, M., 1971, The News and Information Bureau, Broadhurst, personal papers, New South Wales State Library MLMSS41 45

Truth, 25 May 1958, 'Gala Evening for Good Cause'

Walford, L., 1969, 'Palm Trees and Psychedelics', Broadhurst, personal papers, New South Wales State Library MLMSS41 45

Walford, L., 27 June 1971, 'A Film Made of Gold', *Sun Herald*

Walford, L., 'Our Town', Broadhurst, personal papers, New South Wales State Library MLMSS41 45

Watson, L., 2003, *Twentieth Century Fashion*, Carlton Books, London, p 38

Index